RISE BEYOND YOUR FEARS

RESHMA

Chennai • Bangalore

CLEVER FOX PUBLISHING
Chennai, India

Published by CLEVER FOX PUBLISHING 2025

ISBN: 978-93-7500-426-4

Dedication

To every heart that learned to rise again,
and to every soul that loved despite fear —
This book is for you.

To my best friend — who walked into my life in silence
and filled it with the light I needed the most. Your presence
became a strength I didn't know I was missing, and a bond
that showed me what staying truly means.
Thank you for existing.

And to my grandmother —
whose quiet courage shaped the woman I am becoming.
Your strength, wisdom, and unconditional love
have been the foundation of my life.

CONTENTS

EPILOGUE

Every ending is just a doorway.
Every fall reshapes you.
Every moment of courage becomes your legacy.

And when you finally look back from a place of clarity,
you realise that nothing was ever working against you —
it was all preparing you.

Love didn't save you.
You saved yourself.
And love simply matched your new frequency.

PREFACE

Rise Beyond Your Fears

We all arrive at adulthood carrying invisible stories —
stories of love that shaped us,
loss that cracked us open,
fear that held us back,
and courage that slowly pulled us forward.

No one is born fearless.
We learn courage only after walking through life with trembling hands.

This book was not written from a place of perfection,
but from a place of becoming —
from the quiet moments when we choose ourselves,
from the nights we break down only to rise again,
from the soft realisations that healing is not loud… it is patient.

I began writing these pages during a time when everything felt uncertain —
identity, relationships, purpose, even love.
But somewhere between the heartbreaks,
the goodbyes,
the friendships,
the unexpected people who walked into my life,
and the version of myself I fought so hard to meet…
I realised something life-changing:

Fear doesn't end when life gets easier.
Fear ends when *you* get stronger.

Every chapter in this book is a reflection of that strength —
the kind that grows quietly inside you
when the world thinks you're breaking.

This book is not only about romance,
or healing,
or destiny.
It is about the journey of returning to yourself
after losing yourself in people, expectations, and life.

It is about understanding that:

- Love is not what shakes you; love is what steadies you.
- Growth is not loud; it is made of tiny everyday choices.
- Healing is not forgetting; it is remembering without breaking.
- Destiny is not luck; it is alignment.
- And courage is not the absence of fear; it is moving anyway.

If you are holding this book,
maybe a part of you is trying to rise too —
beyond your doubts,
beyond your past,
beyond the old version of you that learned to shrink.

I hope these pages sit with you the way a friend would —
quietly, gently, without judgment.
I hope they remind you that your story is far from over.
And I hope they help you see that the greatest transformation
of your life
begins not when the world changes,
but when **you** do.

This book is a hand extended toward you —
to remind you that you are not alone,
that your heart is far stronger than you think,
and that rising beyond your fears
is not just possible —
it is inevitable
when you choose yourself.

Welcome to the journey.
Welcome to your becoming.

INTRODUCTION

Most people believe life changes through big moments —

a new city,
a new relationship,
a heartbreak,
a miracle,
or a sudden turning point.

But the truth is simpler.

Life changes the day you realise you can no longer live as the old version of yourself.

That moment is quiet.
It arrives without warning.
Sometimes it comes in the middle of a breakdown,
sometimes in the middle of a conversation,
and sometimes in the middle of an ordinary day when something inside you whispers:

"This isn't who I want to be anymore."

This book was born from that whisper.

For years, many of us — including me — lived on autopilot.
We loved blindly, trusted too quickly, feared too deeply, and broke silently.
We carried wounds we didn't talk about,
longings we didn't admit,
and dreams we didn't allow ourselves to pursue.

We fought battles no one saw.
We kept giving even when we were empty.
We held on to people who were not meant to stay.
And somehow, we forgot that our life is our own.

Then one day, something shifts.

Not outside — but inside.

This book captures that shift.

It captures the moment a woman decides to stop waiting for someone to save her,
and starts learning how to save herself.

It captures the truth we avoid facing:

Healing does not begin when life becomes easier.
Healing begins when *you* decide to meet your own strength.

As you turn these pages, you will walk through:

- love that steadied instead of shaking
- friendships that healed quietly
- fears that dissolved slowly
- pain that transformed into power
- and the beautiful becoming of a woman who chose to rise

This is not just my journey.
It is the journey of anyone who ever loved deeply,
lost painfully,
fell apart quietly,
and rebuilt themselves bravely.

The chapters that follow are not instructions.
They are reflections —
pieces of truth, pieces of experience, pieces of soul.

I hope they remind you that:

You are allowed to outgrow people.
You are allowed to choose peace.
You are allowed to want more.
You are allowed to start again.
You are allowed to rise.

And when you rise beyond your fears,
life begins to meet you with a different kind of magic —
the kind that was always meant for you.

This is the introduction not just to a book,
but to **your own becoming**.

Welcome.
Let's begin.

PROLOGUE

The Moment Everything Changed**

There is a moment in every person's life
when the world looks exactly the same…
yet something inside them has shifted forever.

For me, that moment didn't arrive with noise.
It came quietly —
in the stillness of a late night,
standing alone near a window,
watching a city that didn't know my name
and holding a heart that no longer knew who it belonged to.

I remember the heaviness in my chest.
The questions I couldn't answer.
The fear I couldn't explain.
The love I didn't know how to carry
and the pain I didn't know how to release.

I wasn't broken.
But I wasn't whole either.
I was simply a woman standing somewhere between who she had been
and who she was meant to become.

And yet, in that quiet moment,
something inside me whispered a truth I had been avoiding for years:

**"If you do not change your life now,
your life will change you."**

Fear was no longer the enemy.
Waiting was no longer an option.
Love was no longer enough if I wasn't choosing myself too.

That night was not the beginning of my healing,
nor the end of my pain —
but it was the first time I looked at my reflection
and saw someone worth fighting for.

Someone who had survived the storms.
Someone who had stories written on her skin.
Someone who owed herself a new kind of life.

A life built on courage instead of fear.
Growth instead of patterns.
Destiny instead of attachment.
Becoming instead of breaking.

I didn't know then where that moment would lead me —
to new cities,
new friendships,
new love,
new versions of myself.

But I knew one thing with absolute certainty:

My life was about to change
because I was finally ready to change for myself.

This book begins from that moment —
the quiet turning point
between the woman I was
and the woman I would rise to become.

And in that rise,
I found a truth that rewrote everything I believed:

The greatest love stories begin
the day you choose to love yourself first.

Chapter 1

EVERYTHING I ONCE WISHED FOR

Bangalore winters are magical. The air feels soft and cold—the kind that makes you pull the blanket a little tighter and still smile. Outside, the streets are quiet, a thin layer of fog resting on the trees. You can smell filter coffee from some house nearby, hear a scooter going slowly, and sometimes the sound of a dog barking from far away. The sky turns from dark blue to light gold, and the city wakes up in its own slow way—calm and peaceful.

I live in Indiranagar, in a big house—exactly the way I always wanted. Large windows that let the sun in, cream walls, wooden floors that stay cool even in summer, and a long balcony filled with green plants. There's warmth in every corner—my books on the shelf, candles near the bed, fairy lights by the mirror, and soft curtains that dance when the wind blows in. When I was younger, I used to imagine having a house like this. Now I wake up here every morning. It still feels like a dream.

The alarm had been ringing for five minutes before I finally opened my eyes. I smiled. Waking up at 5 a.m. isn't easy, but I made a promise to myself—to give myself good mornings, to take care of my mind and body. I never break my promises.

That's my way of showing love to myself—by doing what I said I would do.

I got out of bed, walked halfway to the door, and turned back. I had forgotten my scrunchie again. It was on the table near my lamp. I tied my hair into a bun and looked at myself in the mirror. "Good morning, Soumya," I whispered.

When I opened the balcony door, cool air rushed to my face. The city still looked half asleep. From the neighbour's house, aunty's Suprabatham was playing. There's something about that song—it feels like the morning itself is praying for you. Everyone at home was still sleeping. I like that—doing my own things quietly while the world is calm.

I spread my mat on the floor and sat cross-legged. Ten minutes of meditation—my best way to start the day. I don't try to stop my thoughts anymore; I just observe them and let them pass. Sometimes I pick one sound—maybe the temple bell or a bird—and keep my focus there for five minutes. It trains me not to run away from focus. It helps me stay steady through the day and gives me space to think before reacting. I'm still learning, day by day. When I finished, I said my affirmations softly: *I am calm. I am grateful. I am safe. I am becoming a better version of myself every day.*

After that, I took out my new Pilates board. I saw a cute Instagram reel last week—the girl looked so happy balancing on it. I ordered it that same night, and now I'm loving it. Just fifteen minutes, and I feel light and strong. The stretch in my body wakes me up better than coffee.

Not every day is the same. Some days it's the gym, some days it's the park for a walk. When my heart calls for it, I go to the park just to talk to new people. I love how much you can learn from short conversations—they always leave me feeling lighter. Maybe that's why people say I have a calm aura. I like hearing that, but more than that, I like feeling it. I've worked hard for this calm.

After Pilates, I decided to try something new—the ice-water face dunking I saw on Instagram. I filled a bowl with water and ice cubes, took a deep breath, and dipped my face in. It was freezing. I laughed out loud. But when I looked up, my skin was pink and fresh. I patted it dry, put on my moisturizer and sunscreen, and smiled. Small rituals make big differences.

Then came my favourite part—coffee. I recently bought myself a small brewing machine. I'm still learning how to use it properly, but I love the sound it makes in the morning—that soft hum while it brews. Until a few months ago, I was more of a green-tea person. In fact, I still am at heart. I drink tea whenever my heart calls for it. But lately, coffee has started to grow on me.

Now that I've started drinking it, I want to learn how to make different kinds—cappuccino, flat white, pour-over—all of it. It's actually on my little bucket list to learn every style one day.

I've always been a loyal Teabox customer; I almost own their whole collection by now. I love trying new green teas, reading about where they come from, and tasting them slowly like small stories in a cup. But ever since this new coffee machine entered my kitchen, it feels like I've found a new kind of peace—the smell of freshly brewed coffee in the air, the warmth in my hands. It just feels like home.

The smell of fresh coffee filled the room. I poured it into my favourite white mug and stepped out onto the balcony again. The fog passed right in front of my face, soft and cool. For a second, I felt like I was living inside a Shekhar Kammula movie—the soft breeze, the peaceful music from the neighbour's house, the warmth of my coffee. It was the kind of morning I always imagined. Now I am Living it.

After my black coffee, I went in to change into my workout clothes. Honestly, I love this part. There's something about wearing new gym clothes that instantly puts me in the mood to work out. I keep buying new ones—cute tops, shoes, even matching hairbands. I tell myself it's for motivation, and honestly, it works.

Today was gym day—leg day, actually. My trainer jokes that it's everyone's least favourite, but I kind of enjoy it. Having a trainer feels nice. He sets up all the machines, adjusts everything, and literally tells me what to do. Sometimes I laugh and say, "I get such princess treatment here, I barely lift a finger!" He laughs too, and it's true—I just sit, do my sets, and chat between them. We usually end up talking about random things—food, music, even funny stuff that happens in the gym. The hour just flies.

After my workout, I drove back home. As soon as I walked in, I could smell breakfast being made. My mother-in-law was in the kitchen, humming some old song while flipping dosas. She has honestly become my best friend these days. It's our little ritual—we sit together in the mornings, have breakfast, and talk about our plans for the day.

And yes, I'm married.

People often ask how I got so lucky to have this kind of bond with her. Honestly, it didn't happen overnight. It took time—a lot of small efforts, patience, and choosing love over ego every single time. But somewhere along the way, we met halfway, and now we just get each other.

Before I left for work, she packed my lunch herself. Our house-help is the sweetest—she helps my aunt so well and makes sure she gets everything without a single complaint. My mother-in-law often says she doesn't even have to remind her of things anymore. Watching them work together so calmly teaches me a lot every single day.

And if you're wondering why I haven't mentioned him yet—well, he's away on a business trip right now. But don't worry, I'll tell you our story soon… how we met, how it all began, and everything that came with it.

The sweetest part? My mother-in-law now waits for me to come home and tell her about my day—just the way she waits for her son. That feeling of being cared for is priceless.

At work, I had a few meetings lined up. It's been a while since I started this company, and honestly, it still feels surreal sometimes. My only goal has always been simple—to create a place where everyone feels safe, supported, and happy. I want people to actually look forward to coming to work.

It took me a long time to reach here. There were days when everything felt too heavy to handle—decisions, deadlines, people, emotions—all of it. Certain things do get difficult sometimes, even now. But with time, experience, and the grace of God, I've learned how to manage it all.

I've realised one thing—when you walk through life with grace and confidence, things eventually fall into place. Maybe not instantly, but they do. You just need to stay calm and trust the timing.

I've made such good friends at work too—people who inspire me, push me to do better, and still make me laugh in between meetings. We've built such a healthy and positive environment that sometimes it doesn't even feel like work. Every day feels like a mix of learning, laughter, and gratitude.

In the evening, my mother-in-law came to pick me up from the office for a little shopping session. Can you believe that? She's honestly the sweetest. We wanted to check out this new mall nearby, and since Arabic food has recently become my favourite cuisine, we planned to have dinner at this new Arabic restaurant that just opened.

We spent hours roaming around, trying new outfits, laughing at random things, and taking pictures like two best friends. By the time we sat down for dinner, we were starving, and the food was so good—I think I've officially become obsessed with Arabic flavours now.

You know, people always say mothers-in-law get insecure after marriage, thinking their sons might change. But in my case, it's actually the opposite—my husband sometimes gets a little jealous because of how close we are. It's kind of cute, honestly. She treats me no less than her own daughter.

And the funny thing is, I think I've been manifesting this kind of relationship for years without even realising it. I remember watching a Korean web series called *Playful Kiss*. I absolutely loved how the hero's mother adored the heroine—the way she got excited about the smallest things, the way she took care of her like her own child. Later, I saw another movie where the bond between the daughter-in-law and mother-in-law was so beautiful. They understood each other, sought each other's approval, almost like best friends.

All those moments got deeply rooted in my mind. I used to think, "That's how I want it to be for me too." And somewhere along the way, that desire shaped the way I approached my own relationship. I took small actions, built trust, and met her halfway with love and understanding—and that's exactly how this bond became real.

Sometimes, I look at her and think—this is exactly how I imagined my life would be. Peaceful, full of love, laughter, and small moments like this. And now, I really do have it all.

Sometimes, when I sit in moments like this—calm, content, surrounded by love—I think of my parents. I know I wouldn't be this person without them. They raised me to think freely, to speak gently, and to always see the good in people. They never forced me to be someone I wasn't—instead, they taught me how to be myself with kindness. That's something I'll always be grateful for.

I've had my share of hurdles, just like everyone else, but the way they brought me up gave me the strength to face them with grace. They taught me to respect every relationship, to understand people rather than judge them—and I think that's exactly what helped me build the kind of life I have today.

We reached home pretty late. I took a quick shower and changed into my comfy clothes—there's something about clean, soft clothes at night that makes me feel instantly relaxed.

I went into the kitchen, opened my tea collection, and picked my favourite chamomile green tea. The smell itself feels like peace in a cup. I made it slowly, just the way I like—letting it sit for a few minutes while the steam filled the room.

I always pour my chamomile tea into a transparent glass. I don't know why, but that's just how I like to have it. There's something about watching the golden colour glow under the light, the herbs slowly settling at the bottom—it makes me feel calm and good inside.

Before heading to the balcony, I called my husband and spoke to him for a few minutes—just a quick catch-up about his day. He's always so busy; I keep teasing him about it. Now you probably understand how I became such good friends with my mother-in-law, right? Since he's busy most of the time, we've spent a lot of time together, and that's how this beautiful bond grew between us.

A few minutes later, I carried my cup to the balcony. The night air was cool, the sky clear, and the city lights shimmered quietly in the distance. I sat down in my favourite chair and took a slow sip. This has become my little night routine—something I do to feel lighter before I sleep. Chamomile has that magic; it tells my mind, "You can rest now. The day is done."

You might think, *Isn't this life too good to be true?* And honestly, I used to think the same. For the longest time, I believed that peace like this was only for certain people—people who were luckier, calmer, or had easier lives. But I was wrong.

This life became real the day I stopped doubting that I deserved it. The moment I truly believed I could have it all—love, peace, success, balance—everything started shifting. It didn't happen overnight; it came slowly, one belief at a time.

I began trusting that even when things didn't go my way, they were still somehow working for me. And that's when the magic began—not from the outside, but from inside me.

Now, I feel safe. I feel peaceful. I feel loved—not because everything is perfect, but because I finally stopped fighting life.

The universe feels like a safe place now, like it's on my side, gently guiding me where I'm meant to be.

I took another sip of tea and looked up—my eyes stopped at a photo on the wall. It was from my college days. I was laughing in that picture, hair messy, eyes bright. But now, when I look at it closely, I can see what I couldn't see then—there was fear behind that smile. Fear of not being enough. Fear of being misunderstood. Fear of losing people I loved.

I didn't realise how long I had been staring at it. Without knowing, I sank into the sofa a little deeper. And just like that—I was back there again.

Back in those college corridors, back with that younger version of me, back to where it all began.

Chapter 2

THE GIRL BEHIND THE SMILE

Back then, I laughed loudly, spoke fast, and thought even quicker. Everything looked fine from the outside, but inside, I was always running behind approval, behind people, behind the idea of being liked.

I was that girl who always wanted a perfect life—especially an ideal relationship. I don't know when it started, but somewhere deep in my heart, I believed that if I ever got into a relationship, it would be perfect. I would play my role beautifully, and it would last forever. That was the fantasy I carried with me.

But little did I know that it takes a lot of courage to hold everything that comes with a relationship. Love is not just about the happy pictures and cute texts; it's about patience, understanding, and a lot of emotional work—something I didn't fully understand back then.

There's a Japanese saying—"Maintenance is always cheaper than repair." No one really knows who first said it, but it's one of those truths that fits everything—a car, a house, even a relationship. What you don't maintain, you eventually lose.

Back then, I didn't realize that love needs attention even when everything feels fine. Most of us start caring more only when things begin to slip away—and that's exactly how we lose what was once perfectly okay.

Anyway, before I go deep into that, let me skip to the good part.

As a child, I was always fascinated by rom-coms. I would sit glued to the TV, watching those dreamy love stories where everything fell perfectly into place—the meet-cute, the confessions, the happy endings. Somewhere deep down, I promised myself that one day, I would have a story like that too.

I knew not everything in movies was real, but a small part of me always whispered, "Maybe it's possible." I never liked how people spoke negatively about relationships. Whenever someone said, "Love doesn't last," or "People always change," I used to ignore it. I didn't want to believe that. I wanted to hold on to positive beliefs—to believe that love could be kind, gentle, and forever.

Not just mine—even when someone around me fell in love, I would get so excited as if it was happening to me. There's something about love stories that always makes me smile. I would sit with my friends, eyes wide, heart full, and say, "Tell me everything!

How did they meet? What did he say first? When did they realize they liked each other?" I wanted to know every tiny detail—every text, every moment.

I think I've always been that person who loves love—who finds joy just in seeing people fall for each other. Maybe that's why I believed love was magical. Not everyone gets to experience it, and when it happens, it feels like a miracle.

And then one day, it happened to me.

Meeting Arjun

It was towards the end of my second year of college when I met Arjun. Until then, I didn't even know he existed. He was from Mechanical Engineering, and I was from CSE.

You know how there's always that silly saying—"Mech and CSE people make the best couples"? I had heard that once, liked how it sounded, and never forgot it.

So when I met Arjun, I smiled to myself and thought, "Maybe this is it."

He came into my life through a mutual friend, just like that—casually, unexpectedly. But his energy felt warm and familiar, like I had known him for a long time.

He was calm, funny, and easy to talk to. I still remember thanking God again and again for sending him into my life.

The way he made me feel was something I can't really describe in words. Everything felt new, light, and exciting. I loved being his girlfriend—saying that word itself made me blush.

When Things Started to Tremble

But after a few weeks, things started to change.

When your entire happiness comes from one place—from one person—even the slightest shake feels like the world is falling apart. If that one source of joy starts fading, life suddenly feels dark. You feel stuck, like there's no way forward.

This is something that happens in almost every relationship.

We start expecting every day to be special. We want our partner to be loving, kind, and patient all the time—just like they were in the beginning.

But love doesn't work like that.

Even the best relationships have days that feel off, quiet, or heavy.

And yet, when it comes to our partner, we hold them to a higher standard than anyone else.

If a friend forgets to call, we understand.

If a family member snaps at us, we forgive easily.

But if our partner forgets to text good morning one day, or sounds distant on a call, suddenly it feels like everything is wrong.

We start overthinking—Did I do something? Is he losing interest?

We don't say it out loud, but inside, we're terrified of what it might mean.

So instead of asking, we keep quiet and suffer alone, scared of what might happen if we bring it up.

When we depend entirely on one person for our happiness, every small thing they do starts to matter too much, if our partner forgets to text good morning one day, or goes for lunch in college without telling us, it suddenly feels like the end of the world.

Most of us instantly think the worst.

Maybe he's losing interest.

Maybe he doesn't care anymore.

And that one thought starts to spiral.

But the truth is—this spiral has power.

When fear and doubt take over, they pull us into low vibration.

And from that place, we start attracting more fear and more doubt.

Have you ever noticed how one small negative thought turns into a whole story in your mind?

You imagine an argument that hasn't even happened yet, or a fight that exists only in your head. You picture him ignoring you, or falling out of love—and suddenly your mood, energy, and peace are all gone.

That's how manifestation works, too—it listens to the vibration you're in.

Fear, doubt, anxiety, control—these are all low frequencies.

Grace, patience, trust, and love—they're high frequencies.

And whichever one you stay in longer, that's what you keep attracting.

But here's the thing I've learned—

If your mind has the power to spiral negatively, it also has the power to spiral positively.

We just haven't practised that side enough.

Your mind is not the enemy —

it's the instrument.

Teach it the music of trust,

and your entire life begins to change.

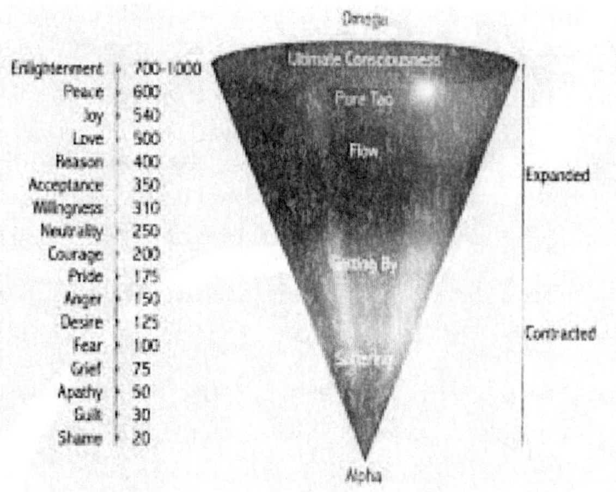

Let's say your partner didn't message you today.

Instead of thinking, *He doesn't care anymore*, what if you paused, took a deep breath, and said to yourself,

"No matter where he is or what he's doing, I know I'm important to him. I trust our connection."

And then you shift your focus.

Do something that lifts your energy—journal, go for a walk, watch something funny, call a friend.

You'll notice that your mind starts calming down.

When the actual situation plays out, you'll handle it so much better. The intensity won't feel the same. You'll see things clearly.

Maybe he just got busy. Maybe he had a group lunch. Maybe it wasn't even a big deal.

I remember one such moment clearly.

Once, Arjun went for lunch with his friends without telling me. I was furious. My face showed it all—I didn't speak, didn't eat, just sat in silence.

That day, I sat alone in the cafeteria, and a girl came and sat next to me. We started talking, and it turned into a really lovely conversation. Over time, she became one of my closest friends.

Had Arjun been there that day, this beautiful friendship would have never happened.

But I didn't realize it then. I spent that whole day angry, carrying unnecessary anxiety, not knowing that the universe was quietly arranging something good for me.

Now, when I think of it, I smile because that's how life works.

If we stay open and calm, the universe gives us gentle gifts—sometimes in the form of new people, sometimes in lessons, sometimes in peace.

I know how it feels when your partner does something that hurts you—it feels like it's going to affect the whole relationship.

But remember, if both of you start vibrating at low energy—reacting with fear, anger, or silence—the relationship begins to lose its spark.

It will never be 50–50 every day.

Some days it might be 70–30, and sometimes even 90–10.

But the calmer, more confident, and more graceful you are, the easier it is to get through those tough moments.

Love doesn't need perfection.

It just needs awareness, patience, and a heart that refuses to give up on kindness—even when things feel shaky.

Now, I know what some people might be thinking—

"If I'm the one who keeps changing and staying calm, won't it become a one-sided relationship?"

But that's the real beauty of grace, and the magic of how the universe works.

When you start vibrating at a higher frequency—with love, trust, and patience—the other person's energy begins to shift too.

It might not happen overnight, but energy is contagious.

When your positive belief is stronger than their fears, it slowly starts to pull them upward.

Your calm becomes their comfort.

Your trust becomes their safety.

And eventually, they start climbing up the same table of higher vibration with you.

That's why choosing awareness and peace isn't weakness—it's leadership in love.

A little more background

Different Worlds

I grew up in a family where love was always given importance. My parents taught me that when you love someone, you love them with all their imperfections. Even before I had a boyfriend, I had this belief deeply fixed in my mind—love is not about finding perfection, it's about choosing someone again and again, despite their flaws.

As I grew up, I always felt confident that if I ever truly loved someone, I could convince my parents for the marriage. I trusted my decisions, and I believed that if I gave my best, everything would eventually work out. That's how I've always been—determined, hopeful, and ready to fight for what I believe in.

But Arjun's upbringing was very different.

And honestly, not just his—I've seen this pattern in many people's lives.

The way we're brought up shapes how we think, how we love, and how much we're willing to fight for what we want.

These days, people often say it's "cool" to be detached or emotionless—not to take love too seriously. And maybe, at that moment, it feels easy. But deep down, everyone eventually wants the same thing—a life filled with love, peace, and understanding.

Arjun came from a very orthodox family. His parents had clear boundaries—they wanted him to marry within the same caste, same religion, same background.

And honestly, I don't see that as "wrong."

They were behaving according to the world they grew up in.

Their thinking was a reflection of their surroundings—of what society told them was "right."

Have you ever noticed this?

Even within the same caste or community, there will be people who support inter-caste or inter-religious marriages, and some who strongly oppose them.

If it were a rule made by caste or religion, shouldn't everyone think the same way?

But they don't.

That's because it's not about caste—it's about conditioning.

It's about what you've heard again and again while growing up.

It's about the thoughts that were repeated so many times that they became beliefs.

Now, just imagine this—if you're someone reading this and you once walked away from love because you thought your parents would disagree, I want you to pause for a moment.

Imagine if your parents had grown up in a world where love marriages were normal.

Where religion, caste, or country didn't matter—only your happiness did.

How different would your story have been?

How many fewer complications would you have had in your life?

The truth is, things change with every generation.

Our grandparents were much stricter than our parents.

They faced hardships and limitations, and that's exactly why they wanted to raise their children with a little more freedom.

If our parents were hurt in love or forced to let go of someone they loved, they tend to become more understanding toward us—because they know that pain.

But if they never faced it themselves, they might never understand it completely.

It's like a cycle—every generation grows a little softer, a little more open-minded, a little more aware.

And I believe that in the same way, we will be more liberal with our children.

Whatever restrictions or fears we are facing now will fade in the next generation.

This isn't about rebellion—it's about standing up for love, just like the gods we pray to did.

Even Parvathi stood against her own father's will to marry Shiva.

She faced resistance, judgment, and pain—but she stood firm because she knew what she wanted.

And today, the same couple is worshipped as the symbol of eternal love.

That's what I mean when I say—God is always with those who fight for what they love.

Because when you move with love, you move with faith.

And when you move with fear, you stay stuck in the same vibration that keeps you away from what's truly meant for you.

So if you ever find yourself scared to fight for love, remember this—

Fear will only create more fear.

But courage, even if it's just one small step, has the power to change generations.

"Let's See Where This Goes"

If you've ever been with someone who's afraid of commitment, you might know this line—

"Let's see where this goes."

It became one of the most-used lines in my relationship. At first, it sounded casual, even romantic—like we were simply going with the flow. But deep down, I wanted clarity. I wanted to feel safe. For a girl who always lived joyfully and confidently, that uncertainty slowly started to scare me.

I had already built a whole life in my head—how we'd grow together, travel, maybe even get married someday. And suddenly, there was this small voice whispering, "What if he leaves?" That's when fear entered my mind.

When I felt that fear, I often thought of stories I grew up with—stories of trust and courage, everyone knows the story of Rama and Sita. They are the example we all think of when we imagine devotion and strength. They left the kingdom, they lost comfort and status, but they stood by each other. Even when Sita was taken, Rama never stopped. He never lost faith in what he was fighting for. He kept his sankalp—his promise and purpose—strong. Because of that, he met people like Hanuman, who became the most significant help on that journey. On the right path, you meet the right people.

Sita, too, never gave in to doubt about Rama's love. That is the kind of trust I mean—not blind hope, but deep, steady faith. When someone truly knows what they are fighting for, they keep moving, trusting the path step by step.

So when people say, "Let's see where this goes," we must ask—is this a gentle way of staying open, or is it a soft way of giving up before you even try? There's a difference.

Saying "let's see" can mean *let's be patient and walk together without forcing the outcome.* But it can also mean *I'm not ready to make a decision, so I'll avoid taking responsibility.* The first is openness; the second is avoidance.

Here's what I learned: you don't need to have the whole life planned, but you do need clarity about the next step. Love grows when both people know the direction—even if the full path isn't visible yet. You don't have to decide everything at once. You need to ask yourself—*What is the next step I will take today?* Then the next, and the next. That step-by-step sankalp builds trust over time.

And remember this—if your mind can spiral into fear, it can also spiral into hope. Instead of thinking, "He might leave," try a slight shift: "I am choosing trust today. I will take this step with courage." Then do something that raises your energy: call a friend, go for a walk, write in your journal. Focus on what you can control: your response, your kindness, your steady actions.

If both people keep lowering into fear, the relationship loses its spark. But if one person keeps rising with calm and clarity, their energy often pulls the other up. That's how change happens—quietly, without drama. It's not about winning or losing; it's about choosing love with purpose.

So "let's see where this goes" should be a brave sentence only when it means, "I'm walking this path with you, and I will do the next thing that grows us." If it's just an excuse to avoid, then it's time for a different question: *What step can we take today to move forward?*

When you act with small, steady faith—when you hold your sankalp and keep showing up—life has a way of arranging the right people and the right moments around you. Trust that. And walk gently, but with a heart that chooses.

Fear Changes Everything

Fear is tricky. It starts small—just one thought. But it grows fast.

Soon, I found myself overthinking every text, every silence, every word he didn't say.

I wanted to fix everything, control everything, and make sure nothing went wrong.

I didn't realise then, but I was lowering my own energy.

The kind of relationship I wanted—full of peace, laughter, trust, and joy—comes from a high vibration.

But fear, doubt, anxiety, and control all come from a low vibration.

The more I worried, the more distant things started to feel.

I didn't understand energy or vibration back then.

I was just scared of losing what I loved.

And honestly, that's a very human thing.

When we're scared of losing something, we try to hold on tighter—but sometimes, that's exactly what pushes it away.

When we start vibrating at a lower frequency in one area of life, it doesn't stay there.

It quietly spreads into everything else—our career, our health, our friendships, our family, even our dreams.

See, every person has a few major areas that make up their life—

career, family, health, wealth, relationships, and friendships.

These areas are all connected through one thing—you.

So when fear sits inside you, it doesn't stay limited to just one area.

It changes how your mind works, how your body reacts, and how you see the world.

Have you ever noticed how when one thing goes wrong—say, a small fight, a failure, or even a bad day—everything else starts to feel heavy too?

That's not bad luck.

It's just energy—one negative emotion slowly spilling into other parts of your life.

It's like getting bitten by a snake.

When that happens, what should you do first?

You give first aid immediately—to stop the poison from spreading.

But most of us, when bitten emotionally, don't stop it.

We sit and cry, replay the moment, and let the poison spread.

That's when one small fear turns into a storm—affecting everything we touch.

So next time, when something goes wrong—when "the snake bites"—try not to let the poison spread.

Pause. Take a breath.

Look around and remind yourself—this is just one area of my life, not my whole life.

Your happiness shouldn't come from a single source.

Because when one thing shakes, you'll still have other pillars that keep you standing strong.

These pillars don't always have to be big things—even the smallest ones count.

A morning walk, your plants, your pet, your work, your parents, your friends, your hobbies—these are all parts of your life that can keep your energy grounded.

When you give value to many areas of your life, one storm can't destroy everything.

That's how balance protects you—and how love, when mixed with awareness, becomes unshakeable.

The Power of Thought

And if you're someone who's on the other side—the person who's scared to commit—I want you to know something important.

Fear doesn't make you a bad person. It just means there's a wound somewhere inside you that still needs healing.

But here's the thing: that fear, if not understood, can shape your entire reality.

You see, most fears are not real events—they're just imaginations of what could go wrong.

Your mind can create a thousand versions of the same situation, and fear always picks the worst one to believe in.

Now let's understand this from a simple science example—something that changed the world of physics forever: The Double Slit Experiment.

Imagine this:

Scientists once did a simple but fascinating experiment to understand how tiny particles—like electrons—behave.

They took a board with two small slits (like two narrow windows) and started shooting electrons toward it.

Now, here's where it gets interesting:

When no one was watching, the electrons didn't behave like tiny balls.

Instead, they acted like waves—spreading out and passing through both slits at the same time.

When they hit the wall behind the slits, they created a pattern—showing that there were infinite possibilities for where each electron could go.

But then, the scientists decided to observe the experiment—they set up a detector to watch what was happening.

And suddenly, the electrons changed their behaviour.

They stopped acting like waves full of possibilities and started acting like solid particles—going through only one slit instead of both.

Everything changed the moment they were watched.

The mere act of observation made the electrons behave differently.

In short, when no one was observing, all possibilities existed.

But the moment someone started observing, only one possibility became reality.

This discovery was called the Observer Effect—

a reminder that what we focus on, we bring into form.

Now think about it in life terms.

Out of infinite possible outcomes for every situation, the one you keep focusing on—the one you observe the most—is what becomes your reality.

If you constantly imagine the worst, your energy starts aligning with that possibility, and life mirrors it back to you.

If you imagine the best—with faith, gratitude, and calm—then that version starts taking shape instead.

We are all made of energy—tiny particles constantly vibrating and influencing each other.

That's why, when one person in a relationship changes their vibration—from fear to trust, from doubt to confidence—it doesn't just change them.

It slowly changes the other person's energy too.

Our thoughts don't end inside our heads. They ripple outward, touching everything and everyone we're connected to.

So if you're someone scared of commitment—stop judging yourself.

Just notice the story your mind is repeating.

Because if you stay stuck in fear, you'll keep attracting the same kind of relationships, the same kind of endings, the same lessons—again and again.

But the moment you decide to change that one thought—from "What if it doesn't work out?" to "What if it turns out better than I ever imagined?"—

Your entire vibration shifts.

And when you shift, life around you starts shifting too.

It all begins with one thought.

The Lesson Repeats Until You Heal

You will keep meeting the same person in different bodies until you learn the lesson.

It might look like new faces, new stories, or new beginnings—but deep down, the pattern stays the same.

And then one day, you catch yourself saying,

"No matter what I do, I never feel truly happy."

That's because happiness doesn't come from changing people or circumstances.

It comes from healing the parts of you that still ache.

When your inner child—that small, innocent part inside you—is still scared, unheard, or unloved, it quietly recreates the same stories again and again, hoping this time they'll end differently.

The truth is, healing isn't about fixing the past.

It's about rewiring your subconscious mind—teaching it that you are safe now, that love doesn't have to hurt, and that you don't have to chase it to deserve it.

Once that happens, everything around you starts to shift.

Either the person you're with begins to change with you—rising to meet your healed energy—

or life gently leads you toward someone who already matches that vibration.

Because when you finally learn the lesson,

the pattern ends.

And what comes next isn't a test anymore—it's peace.

Chapter 3

IDENTITY IS EVERYTHING

My mind was used to spiralling in fear.

For years, I didn't even realise it.

As a child, I grew up hearing things like:

"There's no magic in love."

"In life, you just have to adjust."

"Don't ask for too much — you'll end up getting the opposite."

"Great things don't happen to everyone."

These words came from love, from people who wanted to protect me. But slowly, they became part of how I saw the world.

I grew up believing that asking for "too much" would bring pain.

That love had limits.

That if you dreamed too high, life would humble you.

But somewhere deep inside, there was another part of me — a softer, braver voice — that always whispered,

"No. I'll show everyone how beautiful and magical life can really be."

When Love Becomes Protection

So when I finally fell in love, I carried both voices with me — the scared one and the hopeful one.

I wanted to love deeply, but I also wanted to protect my love from anything that could go wrong.

And that's where things slowly started to twist.

Instead of simply being in love, I started protecting love.

I began overthinking every small thing — every tone, every text, every word he didn't say.

I wanted to make sure nothing went wrong.

But love isn't meant to be controlled.

The more I tried to hold it together, the more it slipped away from my hands.

I started focusing more on the relationship than on myself.

Whenever something felt unusual, instead of sitting quietly and asking what was happening inside me, I instantly tried to fix things outside.

I would think about what he was doing, what others might be saying, and what I could do to make the situation look "okay" again.

But that's the thing — when you keep trying to fix the outside, you ignore what truly needs attention — yourself.

It's like putting makeup over a pimple to hide it.

On the surface, it looks fine for a while, but deep down, the problem persists.

Until you start eating right, drinking enough water, resting, and taking care of your body from within, that pimple doesn't truly go away.

Emotional healing works the same way.

Trying to fix people, situations, or appearances only gives temporary peace.

True healing begins when you start treating the pain inside you.

Protecting what you love is a beautiful thing — but protection must begin with protecting yourself first.

Your peace. Your heart. Your energy.

If you are not at peace within yourself, no matter how much love you give, it will always come from a place of fear.

And fear-based love is exhausting — for both people.

People who are unhappy inside cannot make others happy for long.

You can't pour from an empty cup.

You can only share the love that you have built within.

When you learn to protect your energy — to stay calm, grounded, and aware — you stop reacting from fear and start responding from peace.

And that's when your love starts feeling lighter, purer, and more stable.

Because love doesn't need fixing — it needs healing.

And all healing starts within.

The Lesson Behind the Words

Every relationship has both positive reinforcement and negative reinforcement.

When something goes right and we appreciate it, it grows stronger.

But when we fear losing something and keep focusing on it, that fear grows louder.

I remember one incident very clearly.

One of his friends — someone I never really had a good feeling about — often made comments that didn't sit right with me. I could sense she didn't wish us well.

But he didn't see it that way.

One day, during an argument, he said something that cut deep:

"She's actually better in many aspects. I look up to her."

That one sentence stayed in my head for days.

It felt like a slap — as if I was being compared to someone who didn't even like me.

I couldn't stop thinking about it. I replayed that line over and over again,

and my mind kept whispering, "He will never change. I will never be supported."

At that time in my life, I truly believed that thought.

Only much later in my life did I realise something important.

It was never just about what he said — it was about why I believed it.

The truth is, I got triggered because I already carried an old wound —

the belief that I was "not supported enough."

That thought lived quietly inside me,

and the moment someone said or did something that matched it even slightly,

It rushed to the surface.

Back then, I thought, "He doesn't really care about my feelings."

Later in my life, I understood it differently.

Why should I continue feeling sad because of someone else's conditioning?

His words, his behaviour, his reactions —

They all came from his upbringing, his fears, his emotional capacity.

How someone treats you is a reflection of their emotional maturity,

their level of self-awareness,

and their relationship with themselves — not your worth.

The way a person behaves toward you says more about their inner world

than it ever does about yours.

When I say, "People project what they haven't yet faced within,"

I mean that when people have unhealed emotions, fears, or insecurities,

They often throw them at others without realising it.

For example:

Someone who feels unloved might accuse others of being distant.

Someone who secretly feels unworthy might constantly seek validation or compare themselves to others.

Someone who fears rejection might push others away first.

And someone who hasn't processed their own anger might call others "too emotional."

They're not really reacting to you.

They're reacting to their own reflection — the parts of themselves they haven't yet healed.

So when someone dismisses your needs, pulls away, or reacts harshly —

It feels deeply personal.

But most of the time, it isn't.

You're just seeing the limits of their awareness,

their unhealed pain,

and their current capacity for love or intimacy.

It's not about you.

It's about what's unresolved in them.

This doesn't mean you should excuse hurtful behaviour.

But it helps you see things differently.

Because understanding gives you perspective,

And perspective is what sets you free.

People do the best they can with the emotional tools they have at that time.

Some have learned empathy.

Some haven't.

Some know how to express love.

Some are still learning what love really is.

And once you start seeing people through that lens,

You stop taking everything so personally.

You stop carrying their pain as your own.

You realise it's not rejection — it's reflection.

It's not about your value — it's about their readiness.

There comes a moment in everyone's life when you must decide:

Will you continue carrying the story of what someone did to you?

Or will you release it, rewrite it,

and use that energy as fuel to create the life you truly want?

Later in my life, I chose to rewrite mine.

Because forgiveness isn't about saying, "What you did was okay."

It's about saying, "What you did no longer has power over me."

And that's where healing begins —

not in changing others,

but in freeing yourself.

At that time, I didn't understand this at all.

If his intentions were normal and kind, he would have said things differently — not in a way that hurt.

But the truth is, when you care too much about someone who hasn't yet learned how to care back,

you start creating an imbalance.

Why would he treat me with more value than I was giving myself?

People see you the way you see yourself.

When your inner conditioning says, "I am not supported. I am not loved. I am not enough."

That is exactly what the world mirrors back to you.

At that time, I didn't know this was how things worked.

That's why I kept spiraling in fear.

For the longest time, I gave others the power to hurt me —

to shake my peace over their unhealed parts.

But there's another side to this, too — the other coin we often don't talk about.

Even if he truly felt what he said that day,

Sometimes being kind is better than being brutally honest.

This doesn't mean you should fake it or hide your feelings —

It simply means that unnecessary words, said at the wrong time, can create damage that isn't needed.

We all have thousands of thoughts and emotions running inside us.

Even with the people we love the most — our parents, our friends, our partners —

There are moments when we feel frustrated, irritated, or disconnected.

But those feelings pass.

They don't define the relationship.

That's why emotional maturity is not about suppressing emotions —

It's about knowing when and how to express them.

There's a stage for everything.

When things between two people aren't going well,

Comparing or supporting someone else in that moment isn't honesty —

It's insensitive.

It shows a lack of awareness and grace.

Later in my life, I realised that I, too, was unconsciously doing the same

not through words, but through beliefs.

The negative ideas I carried about myself silently reflected in my reality.

Every time I thought, "I'm not valued," life mirrored situations that made me feel unvalued.

Every time I believed, "I'm not supported,"

I found myself surrounded by people who couldn't support me.

It's a pattern — and it continues until you break it.

That's when I understood something deeply —

Healing isn't about changing others.

It's about changing the energy you bring into the room.

When your inner world becomes calm, loving, and confident,

people around you begin to respond to that vibration automatically.

And those who can't — simply fade away.

Because when you shift your energy, your entire reality shifts with it.

And one day, I asked myself —

"Why did I even let someone affect me this deeply?"

That's when I realised something I had been avoiding all along:

I was broken and vulnerable from within.

I needed healing — not validation.

When your aura is weak, you unknowingly attract situations that match that vibration.

You keep calling in lessons instead of love.

Some people genuinely love,

while others act in the name of love — trying to control, test, or prove something.

And when your energy is low, you start confusing one for the other.

You begin to think that attachment is love and that reassurance is safety.

But once you start healing yourself, the difference becomes clear.

When you raise your vibration — through awareness, gratitude, and inner calm —

You attract love that is pure, stable, and safe.

And the people who aren't meant for your energy anymore?

The universe will gently remove them.

Sometimes it feels painful or unfair in the moment,

but later, you'll see it was protection — not rejection.

Because love has a high vibration frequency.

It cannot live for long in spaces filled with fear, insecurity, or control.

So, what do you do when you face something similar?

When someone says or does something that shakes you —

don't argue, don't fight, and don't run behind them for explanations.

Pause. Breathe. Take some time for yourself.

Ask gently —

"What belief inside me is making this hurt so much?"

You'll find that the pain usually connects to something old —

a childhood moment, a memory, a pattern you never noticed.

Once you find that belief, don't fight it. Rewire it.

Start repeating to yourself:

"I am loved."

"I am supported."

"People understand me easily."

"I am always valued and respected."

Record these affirmations in your own voice —

because when your subconscious hears you saying them,

It begins to believe them faster.

Listen to them every day until they become your new truth.

Watch how, slowly, your energy shifts —

and with it, the way people treat you.

Because when your energy changes, the world has no choice but to adjust.

Fighting or arguing from pain will only pull you deeper into that low vibration.

But choosing peace, choosing grace —

That shifts everything.

That's what being a high-value woman or man really means.

It's not about pride or perfection.

It's about knowing your worth, holding your peace,

and protecting your energy no matter who walks in or out of your life.

Never stop being a good person because someone couldn't value it.

Your kindness, when combined with awareness, becomes your power.

And once your energy is healed,

you'll realise — love doesn't have to be fought for.

It just flows to you.

The Shift Begins Within

Later, through introspection, I realised this wasn't just about him.

This was about me.

Growing up, I didn't always feel like I had people who truly took my side.

Of course, some did — but my mind never focused on them.

It only focused on the times when no one did.

Even when I said things like, "It's fine, I don't care," deep inside, it always hurt.

That belief — that I was someone who never got enough support — quietly became my identity.

And identity is everything.

Your life can only reflect who you believe you are.

If you believe you're not supported, the universe will keep showing you situations that prove that belief true.

One day, later in my life, I decided I didn't want to live like that anymore.

I wanted to change this pattern — from the root.

So I sat down with a notebook and wrote every single thing that had ever hurt me — all the moments that still pinched when I thought about them.

Next to each, I wrote my expectations for the person involved.

And then, against that, I wrote what I believed about myself.

For example:

When I wrote, "My friend never stood by me,"

My inner belief said, "I am not good enough to be chosen."

When I wrote, "My teacher compared me to others,"

My belief said, "I am not as smart as others."

When I wrote, "People make jokes about my looks,"

My belief whispered, "I am not beautiful."

And suddenly, it hit me — what they thought about me and what I felt about myself were the same.

They were only mirroring the version of me I was holding inside.

So, for each painful belief, I began asking myself —

"When did I first start believing this?"

And as I went deeper, childhood memories started surfacing.

Times when people casually commented on my looks, my marks, or the way I spoke.

At times, I laughed it off, pretending it didn't matter.

But it did.

I started believing those words were true.

And that's how I slowly built an identity that said,

"I'm not good enough."

People don't always realise how deeply their words can wound.

They joke, compare, or criticise casually —

But the person receiving it might carry it for years.

Back then, I didn't know what "healing" even meant.

I just thought time would erase the pain.

But time doesn't heal unacknowledged wounds — awareness does.

And the biggest problem?

When you carry those wounds into adulthood,

You unconsciously sabotage good things because deep down,

You don't believe you deserve them.

Even when love comes, you push it away.

Even when support arrives, you doubt it.

Because your subconscious mind is still holding on to that old story.

So, later in my life, the first thing I did was forgive everyone who had ever made me feel small, unseen, or unworthy.

Forgiving isn't easy.

But healing without forgiving is almost impossible.

Imagine you're walking with a backpack full of heavy rocks —

Each rock represents anger, hurt, or resentment.

How long can you keep walking like that?

Now imagine that backpack has a small hole,

and with every act of forgiveness, one rock quietly slips out.

You don't even realise when your bag starts getting lighter.

You just start breathing easier.

That's what forgiveness felt like.

I didn't do it for them.

I did it for me.

Because carrying anger was only hurting me more.

After that, I rewrote everything I wanted to believe about myself.

Every old story, every false belief —

I replaced it with a truth that felt good.

I wrote:

"I am loved and supported by everyone in my life."

"I am beautiful inside and out."

"People respect and value me deeply."

"I am confident, calm, and worthy of everything good."

Then, I recorded these affirmations in my own voice.

Because when your subconscious hears you saying those words, it trusts them faster.

I played them every morning and every night — just five minutes a day.

And during the day, whenever I felt low or anxious,

I would repeat them in my mind like a gentle prayer.

Slowly, things started shifting.

The people around me changed.

The way they spoke to me changed.

And most importantly, the way I spoke to myself changed.

My energy felt lighter.

I started trusting life more.

It wasn't magic — it was rewiring.

I was changing my inner world, and the outer world had no choice but to follow.

This realization came much later in my life.

But if you're reading this now, you can start today.

Whether it's your relationships, your work, or your own sense of peace —

It all begins with the stories you tell yourself.

You don't have to wait for someone else to fix you, or for time to "heal everything."

You can take back that power right now.

Sit down with yourself.

Write it out.

Forgive.

Rewire.

Repeat.

Because your life is always listening to what you believe you deserve.

And the moment you start believing you deserve better —

Everything around you begins to rise to meet that belief.

Chapter 4

NORMALISING PEACE

Coming to my own story—

I never want it to sound like my relationship was only made of painful moments.

Because honestly, there were so many soft, golden memories that made my heart feel full.

There were days when I would sit back and think,

"This is it. This is the life I always imagined."

But I also started noticing something unusual about myself.

Whenever life became *too* calm, *too* peaceful, a tiny worry would quietly creep in—

"I'm so happy right now… what if something goes wrong?"

Sounds familiar?

I'm sure most of us have felt this at some point.

It's one of the most common and silent fears people live with—

the belief that **"good things don't last."**

The moment we become aware of how peaceful life feels, instead of relaxing into it, we start doubting it.

We begin waiting for the disturbance, for the "problem," for something to shake it all up.

And slowly, that fear starts shaping the reality we experience.

I still remember one evening very vividly.

I was on a beautiful call with my boyfriend.

Everything about that moment felt perfect—

the laughter, the ease, the comfort of feeling seen and loved.

And right in the middle of all that, a thought flashed through my mind—

"Can life really stay this good? What if something bad follows this?"

That one single thought was enough to shift my entire energy.

I was no longer fully present in the moment.

Instead of soaking it in, I started guarding it—

as if something unseen was waiting just around the corner to take it away.

Years later, when I consciously began working on my beliefs,

I revisited that exact memory during a journaling session.

I wrote that fear down in my notebook:

"Every time things go well, something bad happens afterwards."

Then I asked myself gently,

"Where did this belief even come from?"

I began listing every incident from my life that matched this idea—

times when I was really happy, and then something unexpected happened soon after.

Very soon, a powerful truth landed in me—

That belief didn't come from some universal rule.

It didn't come from destiny.

It came from **repetition**.

That fear had been replayed in my mind so many times

that it slowly turned into my identity.

And once something becomes identity,

life simply keeps bringing situations that match it.

Here's something I wish everyone understood—

You only **attract** what you've already **normalised** inside.

Everything that exists in your life right now—

your level of peace, the way people treat you, the money you make, the love you receive—

exists because somewhere within, you have accepted it as "normal."

For example,

If you're living in a 3BHK house and earning 1.5 lakhs a month,

it means that, deep down, you've normalised that quality of life.

You believe, "Yes, this is possible for me. I can have this."

But when something feels "too good to be true"—

deep emotional safety, consistent peace, effortless abundance—

Your mind doesn't let you hold it for long,

because you haven't yet normalised that version of life.

So the moment something really good starts happening,

your subconscious quietly whispers,

"Do I really deserve this? Can I really keep this?"

And that doubt slowly lowers your vibration,

pulling you back into your old, familiar pattern.

When this hit me, I made a tiny promise to myself:

"From now on, whenever something good shows up in my life,

I will tell myself—

This is normal. I deserve this. I am safe here."

That one slight shift started changing everything.

Because the moment you inform your mind that peace, joy, and stability

are your **new normal**,

your subconscious begins to accept it as truth.

And once your subconscious believes it—

You stop being scared of the good moments.

You start living them with your whole heart.

This isn't just about romantic relationships.

It applies to every area of your life.

To become a new version of yourself,

many of your old beliefs have to die gently.

You cannot step into a new identity

while still holding on to the energy of who you used to be.

Remember—

You can only feel on the outside

what already exists somewhere inside you.

So fill your inner world with high-frequency emotions—

peace, safety, trust, stability.

Soon, that becomes your natural state,

regardless of what is happening around you.

Think of it like this.

When you snap easily or get angry quickly,

it isn't because someone "made" you angry.

It's because anger is already sitting inside you,

and that situation pressed the button.

Just like how a virus spreads more quickly

in someone whose immunity is low,

emotional triggers hit harder

When your inner stability is weak.

Now imagine every trigger as that "virus."

If your emotional immunity is low,

You'll react immediately, feel drained,

and go into spirals.

But if you've built inner peace,

you may still feel the discomfort—

But you respond more softly, more slowly, with greater awareness.

You might even smile and think,

"This doesn't define me anymore."

Have you ever noticed

how the same situation can make one person aggressive,

another person cry,

and a third person stay completely calm?

That's because each person's **identity** vibrates differently.

For one, anger is the default emotion.

For another, sadness.

And for a few, it's peace.

Those peaceful ones aren't heartless or detached.

They have simply stopped identifying with chaos.

They've chosen—

"This no longer defines who I am."

And that single decision changes everything.

Because identity really **is** everything.

You cannot live a peaceful life

while still calling yourself someone who "always struggles."

You cannot experience soft, steady love

while repeating the story "I'm unlucky in relationships."

You cannot live free

while holding on to the belief

that "good things always go away."

The version of you

who already has peace, love, and emotional stability

already exists.

You don't have to create her from scratch.

You have to normalise her within you—

and become her,

one gentle thought at a time.

Identity Shapes Reality

Identity matters more than we realise.

What you are living right now is not punishment—

It is a reflection.

Who you believe you are

decides the kind of life you experience.

The outside world—what we call "reality" or "3D"—

It is nothing but a mirror

showing you the version of yourself

You are currently identified with.

If you see yourself as loved, respected, and chosen,

people around you will *naturally* start treating you that way.
If you see yourself as ignored, unworthy, or unsupported,
your world will keep reflecting situations
that make you feel exactly that—again and again.
You are treated the same way
you treat yourself in your own mind first.
I used to see myself
as someone who was "never truly supported."
So what happened?
Life kept sending me scenarios
That confirmed that story.
It wasn't the universe punishing me.
It was simply mirroring my belief.
That's how energy functions.
That's how identity quietly shapes everything.
Your identity even decides
Which version of your partner do you experience?
Just like there are infinite versions of you—
confident, insecure, peaceful, triggered, hopeful—
There are also infinite versions of *them*.
The version of your partner
who loves you deeply, shows up for you,
and makes you feel safe and seen

already exists.

You don't have to chase them into becoming that person.

You don't have to force it out of them.

You have to tune into the frequency of that version—

by becoming the version of **yourself**

who naturally receives that kind of love.

When you shift your identity,

Their behaviour starts shifting on its own.

When you stop identifying as

"the one who always gets hurt,"

and begin identifying as

"the one who is loved with ease,"

Your world slowly rearranges itself

to match that identity.

You don't have to wrestle your reality to the ground.

You have to become

the version of you

who already lives the life you desire.

That's how you change your mind.

And that's how you change your life.

Becoming the New Version of You

When I say,

"You have to start *being* a new person."
Many people think I'm talking about
"fake it till you make it."
But this is not about pretending.
It's not about wearing a confident mask
when you're breaking inside.
It's not about forcing a smile
when what you really need is rest and tears.
It's about **embodiment**—
gently shifting into the person you want to be,
until that way of being feels natural.
There's a vast difference between faking and embodying.
Pretending feels heavy and tiring—
like acting in a role that doesn't belong to you.
Embodying feels softer—
more like remembering who you were
before life convinced you that you were small.
Imagine this for a moment:
If you *already* believed,
with your entire heart,
that you were deeply loved and valued—
Would you still chase after people?
Would you still go into panic mode

When someone didn't reply for a few hours?

Would your self-worth crash

Every time someone behaved a little differently?

You wouldn't.

You'd breathe.

You'd trust.

You'd remind yourself,

"Someone's silence does not decide my value."

That version of you—

the calm, grounded, secure one—

already exists within.

You don't have to create her.

You have to **return** to her.

She is you

who existed before fear,

comparison,

And self-doubt entered the room.

Before someone's words

made you question your brightness.

Before you started shrinking yourself

to make others comfortable.

She's still there—

waiting for you to come back home to her.

And the day you step fully into that version—
not halfway, not only on good days,
but as a lifestyle—
Everything starts shifting.
Your energy changes first.
And when your energy changes,
The world around you doesn't know
What else to do
except respond.
The same people
begin treating you differently.
The same situations
start feeling less intense.
The same partner
may suddenly seem more secure,
more expressive,
more steady.
Why?
Because you're no longer acting from lack.
You're operating from a place of peace, faith, and self-respect.
That's the power of energy.
That's the power of identity.
And that's how love truly heals—

not by forcing change in others,

But by restoring balance

inside yourself.

Let Me Explain This in a Simpler Way

Imagine you want to build your dream home—

the way you imagine

building your dream relationship.

The moment you decide,

"Okay, I want this kind of house,"

Does it appear the next day?

Of course not.

You start by choosing the land—

a place that feels safe,

comfortable, and right for you.

Then you design the structure,

sort out your finances,

and lay down the foundation.

The foundation is the most crucial part.

If it isn't strong,

no matter how beautiful the house looks from the outside,

It won't feel stable on the inside.

Then the structure is built

step by step—
floor by floor,
room by room.
Slowly, you see it coming to life.
You watch the walls rise,
the doors being fixed,
the windows opening to the sky.
After that comes the interior.
You pick colours that feel warm and inviting.
You select curtains that let in gentle light.
You place plants, candles, cushions—
things that make that space feel like *yours*.
You do all this out of love—
because you know
This is the space where
You will live,
rest,
heal,
and feel safe.
Now imagine trying to live inside that house
while it's still under construction—
no proper walls,
open roof,

dust everywhere.

For a day or two,

your excitement might carry you.

But eventually, you'll feel suffocated, exposed, and restless.

That's exactly what happens in relationships.

If your inner home—

your identity, your self-worth, your sense of safety—

hasn't been built yet,

Love will never fully feel peaceful.

You cannot expect constant peace

from a relationship

when the foundation inside you

It is still shaking.

You'll keep checking,

"Are they still there?

Do they still love me?

Did I do something wrong?"

Because of the belief,

"I am safe, I am loved, I have enough."

has not yet been cemented inside.

So the work is this:

Build your inner house first.

Brick by brick.

Belief by belief.

Lay down the foundation with self-worth—

reminding yourself

that you are deserving of love

simply because you exist.

Raise the walls of trust—

not blind trust in other people,

But trust in yourself

and in the universe.

Paint those walls

with kindness and compassion—

the same softness

You so easily give to others

but rarely extend to yourself.

Fill that inner home

with gratitude,

joy,

and small rituals that make you feel safe.

This process is not instant.

Just like any real construction,

It takes time.

There will be days

when it feels like the foundation is cracking,

days where nothing seems to be going "right,"
days when you feel like tearing it all down and starting over.
But those days
are exactly the days
You are closest to stability—
because something old is leaving
So something new can be built.
Keep building.
Keep choosing yourself.
One day,
You'll look within and realise—
"My heart finally feels like home."
And when your own heart feels like home,
Your relationships begin to mirror that energy, too.
Love stops feeling like something
You need to fight for or prove.
It becomes something
that flows more naturally.
Because once you become
the version of you
who already feels safe and loved,
You stop chasing peace—
You **become** peace.

Becoming the New Version

So if you truly want your love story to shift,

You have to become the version of yourself

who already lives that story.

When you embody the energy of being loved, supported, chosen, and safe,

the universe—and everyone in your life—

starts responding to that vibration.

The quickest way

to change a relationship

is to stop staying loyal

to the version of yourself

who doesn't believe it's possible.

The moment you choose

a new identity—

one that already has the love, peace, and stability you desire—

Your world begins rearranging

to match it.

It isn't magic.

It's alignment.

Because your reality

will always reflect who you **are**—

not just what you say you want,

not just what you write in your journal,

but what you truly, deeply

believe yourself to be.

Love cannot thrive inside a half-built home. So build yourself first.

Strengthen your foundation. Paint your inner walls love, gentleness and light. And then watch as everything and everyone around you

slowly begins to reflect the same peace

you've lovingly created within.

That is the power of identity. That is the power of awareness.

And that is where real, lasting love begins—

not by changing *them*,

but by finally coming home to **you**.

Chapter 5

TRUSTING THE PROCESS

If you ask me what the most challenging part of healing is, I won't say forgiveness or letting go.

It's *trusting the process.*

When things don't go as planned, when the future looks uncertain, when nothing makes sense — staying calm through all that feels impossible.

And for me, this was the biggest roadblock of all.

I wasn't scared of commitment.

I wasn't scared of love.

I wasn't even scared of fighting for what I believed in.

What scared me most was *the unknown.*

Not knowing how things would unfold.

Not knowing whether the person I loved would still choose me tomorrow.

It's strange — I fell in love with so much courage, yet the uncertainty of it all almost broke me.

I didn't know what "trusting" truly meant.

The Illusion of Control

Whenever something went wrong — a fight, a misunderstanding, a sudden silence — my whole body would go into panic mode.

My heart would race.

My mind would start spinning stories — *"What if this is the end? What if everything falls apart?"*

And in that chaos, I'd react.

I'd say things I didn't mean, cry endlessly, and then blame myself for overreacting.

That's the irony of control — the more you try to hold on, the faster things slip away.

Looking back, I realise — I was never afraid of losing love.

I was afraid of losing *certainty.*

If your peace depends on everything going right, that's not peace — that's control.

True peace is when you can stay calm even when things don't make sense.

Learning to be steady in uncertainty — that's where real growth happens.

When you face constant stress and uncertainty, your body learns to live in survival mode.

You stay alert, tense, and exhausted — always waiting for the next thing to go wrong.

Even in moments of calm, your mind doesn't relax.

And it's not because you're overreacting — it's because your nervous system has forgotten what safety feels like.

That's why learning to calm your nervous system is so important.

It's not just emotional control — it's *energy realignment.*

When you learn to regulate your emotions, you stop reacting from fear and start responding from awareness.

Never let your emotions take complete control of you.

When you stay grounded in chaos, when you walk with grace even when your world feels shaky — that's true strength.

People who stay calm and composed in the most difficult situations are not emotionless;

They're emotionally wise.

They know that reacting won't fix anything — but staying centred will eventually guide them to the answer.

How to Trust When You Don't Know What's Happening Behind the Scenes

One of the hardest things in life is learning to trust when you don't know what's happening behind the scenes.

That's where most of us struggle.

Let me explain it this way —

When you order something from Amazon, you trust that it'll reach you.

You don't call customer care every hour to check if it's on the way.

You don't keep refreshing the tracking page every five minutes.

And imagine if you actually did that — how exhausting would it be?

Would you have any energy left to do other things in your day?

Would you still feel calm or excited about your order arriving?

Of course not. You'd feel tired, anxious, and restless.

Now think about what happens when your next order comes along.

You'd place it with that same energy — worried, impatient, and unsure.

That's exactly how most of us live life.

We've already told the universe what we want — love, peace, success, stability —

But instead of trusting, we keep checking, doubting, and worrying.

That's what I used to do too.

I kept calling the "delivery partner" — the universe — with my fears.

But when you trust, you relax.

And when you relax, life flows.

That's when the magic happens.

The Universe Has a Mother's Heart

The universe has a mother's heart — gentle, patient, and endlessly loving.

It wants to give you what your heart desires.

It never withholds blessings out of punishment or neglect.

The only reason we sometimes don't receive what we want is that we haven't yet built enough *evidence* within ourselves to believe it's possible.

When things fell apart in my life, and I found it hard to trust again, I tried something simple.

I took a notebook and listed down everything that had ever worked in my favour — even the most minor things — from my childhood till now.

Next to each memory, I wrote one thing I noticed:

For all of these, I had less attachment.

I wanted them, yes — but I wasn't desperate.

I didn't put them on a pedestal.

And that's when it hit me —

Every good thing that came into my life came easily because I wasn't chasing it.

I believed it was possible, but I didn't make it my whole reason to be happy.

When I think of it now, I realise — the universe loves just like a mother does.

When we were little, remember how our moms would make our favourite snacks?

Sometimes she'd say, *"Finish your homework first, then I'll give it to you."*

It wasn't to punish us — it was to teach patience and effort.

Fathers do the same —

"When you score well, you'll get that new toy."

And as kids, we'd try harder, not out of fear, but because of the excitement of that reward.

I still remember how my father used to bring me small gifts every evening when he returned home.

On days he came late, I'd wait near the door, half-sleepy but full of hope.

And because I knew he'd bring something for me, I used to behave better that day — finish my homework, help mom, do everything without a complaint.

That little excitement made me want to be better.

Sometimes I'd get a gift after crossing a small hurdle,

and sometimes, just for nothing, just because he loved me.

That's exactly how the universe loves too.

Every time you pass a test, the universe gives you a small reward.

It might not always be the big thing you asked for,

but it's preparing you for it —

just like parents prepare their children to handle bigger responsibilities.

You might wonder, *"Why can't the universe just give me what I want right away?"*

Because the universe knows the life you'll have *after* getting what you want.

And to live that life fully, you need to become emotionally and spiritually ready for it.

It's not delay — it's divine preparation.

Let me give you a beautiful example.

When Lord Rama's army — the *Vanara Sena* — decided that Hanuman would go to find Mother Sita,

The journey wasn't simple.

Many of us imagine that Hanuman just leapt to Lanka and found her easily.

But the truth is — his path was filled with tests.

He was tested again and again by gods and goddesses,

not to stop him, but to *prepare* him.

Every challenge strengthened him,

every obstacle tested his faith,

and every divine encounter made him more resilient.

Because the universe knew what awaited him in Lanka —

the demons, the dangers, the test of his courage.

Hanuman never complained, never stopped.

He kept one thing in his heart —

"I have to unite Rama and Sita."

That clarity of purpose carried him through every storm.

He didn't see those challenges as punishment.

He saw them as steps — as divine training for his mission.

And that's what the motherly love of the universe looks like.

It doesn't always give you what you want right away —

because it's busy making you *ready* to hold it.

Sometimes it gives, sometimes it delays,

sometimes it even takes away —

But only to give you something more stable, something you can truly keep.

The motherly love of the universe may not always be visible,

but it's always there —

working quietly, protecting, preparing, and aligning everything for your highest good.

So whenever life feels uncertain,

Whenever things seem delayed,

just remember —

You're not being ignored, you're being prepared.

And one day, when everything you asked for finally arrives,

You'll look back and whisper,

"Now I understand why it took time."

The Root of All Imbalance

If I had to trace every single problem I ever had in a relationship — whether it was misunderstanding, overthinking, or fear — it would all lead back to one truth:

We put the people we love on a pedestal.

Most of us don't even realise when we do it.

It starts so innocently — we admire them, we value them, we start seeing them as the most essential thing in our lives.

Slowly, they become our source of happiness, our reason to smile, and our sense of safety.

And in that process, we unknowingly hand over our power.

When you put someone or something on a pedestal, you automatically lower your own vibration.

You start looking up to them, and naturally, anything placed higher will look down on you.

It's not that they are "better" or that you don't deserve them —

It's simply that you've started believing they hold more power than you do.

You've unconsciously told the universe,

"This person is greater than me. I can only be happy if they choose me, love me, or stay with me."

And the universe, being the loving mother it is, will never let you settle in a state where you see yourself as less.

It will wait — patiently, tenderly — until you raise your vibration to match what you desire.

Because you can only attract what you are aligned with.

The Frequency of Alignment

Let's make it simple.

Imagine trying to call your friend whose number is **123**, but you accidentally dial **124**.

No matter how many times you press "call," your friend won't pick up — not because they don't want to,

but because you're simply not on the right frequency.

The same happens in life.

Your desires — love, peace, success — vibrate at the frequency of gratitude, trust, and calm.

But if *you* are vibrating with fear, doubt, or desperation, the call doesn't go through.

And that's where so many of us get stuck.

We think we're doing everything right — caring deeply, loving truly, trying our best —

But energetically, we're dialling the wrong number.

When you put something on a pedestal, you start overworking for it.

You overthink every message.

You overgive in every situation.

You overexplain just to be understood.

And you overexhaust yourself just to keep something you were meant to receive effortlessly.

It's like constantly tracking your Amazon package —

refreshing the page every few minutes,

checking every little update,

calling customer care when there's a minor delay.

How tiring would that be?

Would you have any energy left for other parts of your day?

Would you even enjoy the moment when the package finally arrives?

No. You'd be too drained.

And the same thing happens in love —

You chase so hard that when it finally comes, you're too exhausted to receive it with peace.

Making the Process Simple

Here's the truth that changed everything for me:

Manifestation — and love — aren't meant to be tiring.

They're meant to be peaceful.

You're not supposed to beg for what's already yours.

You're meant to align, trust, and allow.

When you stop forcing things and start trusting the natural rhythm of life,

you save energy — emotional, mental, and spiritual.

That calmness naturally raises your vibration to the level where your desires already exist.

So, the next time you find yourself spiralling in doubt or fear, pause for a moment.

Take a deep breath and remind yourself:

"I've already placed my order.

I trust it's coming.

I am worthy of everything I desire."

Because you are.

And the moment you stop chasing,

what's meant for you starts finding its way —

quietly, softly, and always right on time.

Trust Even When It Doesn't Make Sense

But here's the most challenging part: trusting when nothing makes sense.

Trust doesn't mean everything will go your way.

It means believing that *even when it doesn't*, it's still working for you, not against you.

Sometimes the delay is protecting you from something that isn't ready.

Sometimes the rejection is redirecting you to something better.

Sometimes the silence is giving space for something new to grow.

You might not see it now,

but the universe is constantly rearranging things behind the scenes —

moving people, opportunities, and timing to serve your highest good.

You have to trust so deeply that even when everything looks uncertain, you can still whisper:

"This is happening exactly as it's supposed to.

God is still on my side."

That's what real faith looks like.

Not the kind that needs proof,

but the kind that simply *knows* you're being guided.

Because the universe doesn't respond to panic — it responds to energy.

And when your faith becomes unshakable,

the universe has no option but to align everything in your favour.

So, no matter how dark it feels,

no matter how unsure the path seems,

trust that you're being led to something you once prayed for.

Every detour, every delay, every heartbreak —

none of it was punishment.

It was all preparation.

And one day, when everything unfolds perfectly,

you'll look back and say,

"Now I understand. That's why it took time."

In the End, Trust Wins

Trust isn't built in a day.

It's built every time you choose calm over chaos.

Every time you say, *"I don't understand this, but I trust it."*

Every time you walk through fear and still keep your heart open.

That's what makes you strong.

That's what makes your love divine.

Because when you trust, you stop chasing and start allowing.

And in that surrender, you finally meet peace —

the peace that was meant for you all along.

How the Universe Works

What I've learned now is that the universe doesn't understand "past" or "future."

It only responds to how you're feeling *today.*

It reacts to your *current energy.*

If your heart is full of fear, the universe will keep sending you more reasons to fear.

If your heart is full of trust, it will give you more reasons to trust.

That's why my relationship started shaking —

not because Arjun changed, but because my vibration did.

One day, when everything seemed perfect, everything changed.

Out of nowhere, Arjun left my life.

It was so sudden — almost unreal.

It felt like when a movie ends and the director says *"Cut,"*

and the actor walks out of character as if it never existed.

He didn't discuss it with me.

He just decided — and left.

If you ask me even today, I don't know why he did that.

There was no big fight, no final conversation, no closure.

He just disappeared.

People around me had their own versions of the story —

"He never really loved you,"

"He cheated,"

"He got bored,"

"It was just a phase."

I heard them all.

And for a long time, I believed them.

As a woman, I faced the backlash, too.

People started talking, judging, and labeling me with stories I didn't deserve.

Everyone had something to say — except him.

I waited for him to come back.

Days turned into weeks, weeks into months.

But he never did.

And for the first time in my life, I felt like my whole world had ended.

It was as if someone had turned off the light inside me.

I lost direction.

I cried every single day.

And there were moments — dark, painful moments —

When I even thought of ending my life.

Because when your entire happiness comes from one person,

Their absence feels like death.

But here's the truth I learned the hard way —

Sometimes God removes people not to punish you,

but to protect you from what you can't yet see.

At that time, I didn't understand it.

I kept asking, *"Why me?"*

But my Krishna had already seen what I couldn't.

He knew that this chapter had to end for something far better to begin.

Finding Meaning in the Pain

It took me months — maybe even years — to truly rise again.

But one day, I made a conscious choice to stop asking, *"Why did he leave?"*

And I started asking instead, *"What is this trying to teach me?"*

That question changed everything.

I realised something quietly but clearly — I wasn't angry anymore.

In fact, I couldn't be.

Because if I hadn't walked through that pain, I would have never discovered my worth, my strength, or the depth of self-love that now lives inside me.

He was never my mistake.

He was my greatest mirror.

And even though we never spoke again,

He will always hold a space in my story —

not as the man who broke me,

But as the one who unknowingly helped me rebuild myself.

I don't know what happened to him after that.

I don't care what people say or what the truth is.

The only thing that matters to me is the choice I made — to forgive him.

And the moment I truly forgave, something shifted inside me.

I felt lighter.

The heaviness that had lived in my chest for so long slowly began to dissolve.

Forgiveness didn't mean I agreed with what he did.

It simply meant I stopped carrying the weight of it within me.

Sometimes I wonder — had I been the woman I am today back then —

calmer, wiser, more grounded — maybe things would have unfolded differently.

But even then, I remind myself: everything happened exactly the way it was meant to.

Because every experience, especially the painful ones, shaped me into the person I am today.

Today, I can say this with a full heart —

it was his loss, not mine.

But it was also my awakening.

The love I gave was real. It was pure.

And pure love never goes to waste.

It always returns — maybe not from the same person, but from life itself, multiplied.

Yes, he left.

For whatever reason.

For whoever it was meant to be.

But I know one truth with complete certainty —

that day, even when it felt like I lost everything,

Life was still working in my favour.

Because that was the day I stopped searching for love outside

and slowly began finding it within myself.

The Hardest Part of Leaving

Leaving was the hardest thing I had ever done.

Not because I didn't know what I was losing —

But because I didn't yet understand what all I had already lost *by staying.*

And it's not just me.

So many people stay in relationships without realising what they are losing —

their self-worth, their voice, their peace —

because they are scared.

Before he finally left, life had given me countless chances to walk away.

Again and again, I was shown signs.

But I stayed.

Because I am a fighter.

And he was not.

At that time, I didn't understand the subconscious patterns I was living through.

I didn't see the quiet compromises.

I didn't recognise how much of myself I was shrinking.

But today, with all the clarity life has given me, I know one thing for sure:

With a fighter's spirit, a pure heart, and the courage to grow —

You will always end up with greater things.

Some relationships are not meant to grow with you.

Some chapters are meant to end exactly on the day they end.

And yes — sometimes, life may bring the same person back in a different role,

only if it serves your evolution.

Otherwise, their purpose is already complete.

Through all the pain, I realised one powerful truth:

I gave all the love I could.

My love was pure.

I did the best I knew how to do at that time.

I may not have understood my subconscious mistakes back then,

but I am sure of this —

When your love is pure,

Life will always reward you in multiple ways.

Always.

Some of you may quietly wonder this:

"If this is what you honestly asked for…

If your love was pure…

Then why didn't you get Arjun?

Was giving up the only option?"

And this is my honest answer.

At one point, Arjun and I were no longer a **vibrational match**.

Not because our love was fake —

But because my inner world had become filled with fear, doubt, and emotional imbalance.

The negative voices inside me had started speaking louder than love itself.

And love cannot survive in a space like that.

Love cannot live in an **unfinished house** —

a space that is still under construction,

where the foundation is shaking,

where safety is not yet built.

And this truth applies not just to relationships before marriage —

It applies even after marriage.

You must have seen it too.

So many couples stay together, yet fight every day.

They complain, fear, doubt, and live in emotional chaos.

Sometimes what keeps them together is not love at all —

but children, society, expectations, or financial dependency.

They remain together because they are married.

Not because they are at peace.

In my case, that wasn't the path meant for me.

Because a relationship cannot survive

when only one person is trying to heal it.

Love is not a solo effort.

It requires **mutual awareness, mutual effort, and mutual growth**.

At that time, I was not this aware.

I was not this emotionally mature.

And neither was he.

I was trying to repair something

from a place of fear and attachment,

not from clarity and inner stability.

And when only one person repairs,

the structure never truly holds.

So no —

I didn't "lose" him.

And I didn't "give up."

What actually happened was this:

I outgrew a version of myself

that was surviving on fear instead of love.

Sometimes, the universe doesn't remove people because you failed.

It separates you because you are being prepared for a **higher, healthier alignment**.

And today, with all the awareness life has given me, I can say this gently and truthfully:

Arjun and I were meant to meet.

But we were not meant to remain

in the versions we were becoming.

And that, too, is love.

Not the kind that stays.

But the kind that awakens you.

And maybe, in the future,

If this relationship is truly meant to find its way back in any form,

This person may re-enter my life in a **different role**,

at a **different stage**,

when both of us have healed, grown, and truly become a **vibrational match** again.

Maybe not as lovers.

Not as partners.

But perhaps as **great friends**,

as silent supporters,

as two souls who once loved deeply and now understand each other with peace.

And maybe…

We might never meet again.

Because sometimes, people only meet us

until the lesson is complete.

Yet one truth remains untouched —

What we shared was real,

because we had so much in common,

so much emotion,

so much depth.

And love…

love always finds its way back —

not always in the same form,

not always in the same role,

but in **multiple forms and ways.**

And sometimes,

It returns in a way that feels even **more peaceful, more aligned, and more beautiful**

than what you once imagined.

Chapter 6

WHEN THE WORLD LOOKED DIFFERENT

When Arjun left, everything suddenly felt empty.

It was as if I had been living in a cocoon — soft, protected, and unaware of the world outside.

For so long, my days revolved around one person, one voice, one routine, one heartbeat.

And when it was gone, I didn't know what to do with myself.

When I finally stepped out of that cocoon, the world looked different.

The same streets looked louder, the same people looked busier, and even the air felt colder.

I felt like I was watching life move while I stood still.

I realised something profound —

When I was in my so-called magical wonderland, I never really paid attention to the rest of the world.

I was so caught up in *us* that I forgot *me* — and everyone else.

And when I finally opened my eyes, I saw how many people were walking around just like me —

carrying their own stories,

their own scars,

Their own fears.

Everyone seemed to be fighting silent battles.

Some looked strong but were broken inside.

Some smiled widely but had tears they never showed.

And everyone — in one way or another — was afraid.

The Age of New Labels

When I started to observe people and listen to their stories, I kept hearing new terms —

Situationships. Casual relationships. Ghosting. Benching. Breadcrumbing. Orbiting. Haunting.

At first, I thought these were random slang words,

But when I understood them, I honestly felt sad.

Each of these words was just a fancy way of describing *confusion, fear, and detachment.*

I remember sitting back and thinking —

When did love become this complicated?

When did something so pure start sounding like a game with tricks and rules?

People these days give their fear new names to make it sound sophisticated.

But the truth is simple —

These are just ways of saying, "I'm scared to love deeply."

The Fear of the Unknown

People are scared to love because they fear losing.

Scared to trust because they are scared of pain.

Scared to commit because they don't trust the unknown.

Every day, we meet people who make us feel something special —

Someone who makes us smile a little wider,

Feel calmer, lighter, or truly seen.

But the moment that spark appears, the mind begins to whisper:

"What if this doesn't last?"

"What if I get hurt again?"

So instead of leaning in, we pull back.

Instead of calling it love, we call it "casual."

Instead of trusting the feeling, we start planning an exit.

We think we're being careful, but in truth, we're being fearful.

We've built a world where people are afraid to be

too kind,

too honest,

Too invested.

So we float in the grey —

Not fully in, not entirely out.

But tell me… has playing safe ever truly protected anyone from pain?

Even when you choose "safe," life still finds a way to surprise you.

Every relationship needs a battle —

Either before it begins, after it begins, or sometimes both.

Because it is not easy to stay with a person once you truly know them.

We love our parents and family for this very reason —

Because we share life with them.

They don't judge us for our existence, even if they judge us for other things.

That acceptance came from time, not from impressions.

In the beginning, everything feels beautiful.

Because we only know a few pieces of the person.

But how can you define a whole life?

after meeting someone for three hours

Or even after knowing them for one or two months?

A person is made of all the years they have lived —

Their pain, patterns, habits, fears, memories.

It takes years to know someone truly.

And somewhere in the middle of that journey,

Interest fades — not because love wasn't real,

But because no life is endlessly exciting.

At the end of the day, most of us return to the same routines,

The same tired evenings, the same ordinary silence.

People don't stop loving because love disappears.

They fail because fear grows louder than the heart.

Fear of the unknown.

Fear of what others might think.

Fear of how they will be seen.

Image becomes more important than truth.

So the heart wants one thing,

But actions follow one another.

And in the process,

We don't cheat anyone else —

We cheat ourselves.

How long can a person live like that?

If you fight for who you love,

There will always be a battle —

With circumstances, with timing, with people, with yourself.

If you give up and compromise too easily,

You will still fight —

or to find love again,

Or to live with the emptiness of not choosing it.

At the end of the day,

Compatibility is not something you find —

It is something you build.

Try living without impressing.

Without performing.

Without pretending.

And see how someone falls in love with the real you.

All the great personalities you admire in your life

are nothing like you —

And that is exactly why they inspire you.

There Is No True Certainty

We act like commitment is the only thing in life that's uncertain.

But tell me — what in life is truly certain?

Do you know how long you'll live?

Do you know what will happen tomorrow?

None of us does.

The job you have, the business you're building,

The home you live in — none of it is guaranteed to last forever.

And yet, you show up for it every single day.

Then why do we treat love so differently?

We spend our lives working for money,

chasing success,

Making plans for a future that isn't promised.

But when it comes to love —

The one thing that actually nourishes the soul —

We hesitate.

All because of fear.

The fear of what our parents will say.

The fear of society's judgment.

The fear of not fitting into the image people have built for us.

And because of this fear,

We either end up hurting the person who loved us the most,

Or hurting ourselves by walking away from something pure.

We forget one simple truth:

Love isn't the problem. Fear is.

Winners Don't Play Safe

When you step back and observe life,

You realise most people are not truly living —

They are managing.

Managing their image.

Managing their fears.

Managing their emotions.

But the people who change the world,

The ones who actually live —

They are the ones who take risks.

Those who follow their hearts,

Even when the world calls them foolish.

Winners don't play it safe.

They take a step forward when others step back.

They create paths where none existed before.

If you wait for society's approval before loving someone,

You will wait forever.

You are not meant to fit in.

You are meant to stand out.

A cousin of mine was in love.

But because of society's image,

Because of fear of what relatives might say,

He gave up on the girl he loved — for them.

He let go of that love, not because it was wrong,

But because fear was stronger.

Life moved on.

The same relatives who pressured him earlier

Then started showing concern:

"Poor thing, he isn't finding the right match. We should help him."

Eventually, a match was found.

Just to cope with life and move forward,

He began trying to adjust, to be kind to her, to treat her well.

And suddenly, the same relatives began to judge again:

"Even before marriage, he's doing so much for her… is this necessary?"

How strange, isn't it?

Later, they got married.

And today, even after choosing what society wanted,

They are still not happy because of compatibility issues.

Now, once again, the same people are ready with sympathy.

The truth is —

People wait for such things to happen in your life.

And even when you choose someone by *their* choice,

They will still never be truly happy with who you are

Or for your happiness.

That is when I understood something deeply and clearly —

I must value my own emotions more than anyone else's opinions.

The Only Truth That Matters

In life, we always have a choice:

Who we listen to.

Who we prioritise.

Who we allow into our inner world.

Life is nothing but the choices we make

In the time we are given between birth and death.

The more heartfelt and honest our choices are,

The more fulfilled our life becomes.

We always have the power to decide.

Who gets access to our life and our peace?

Because one thing is certain:

Around negative energy, we can never truly grow.

Faith in the Battlefield

Let us take an example: in the *Kurukshetra war*, Arjuna was paralysed by fear.

He didn't want to fight his own people.

He was shaking, lost, and unsure.

That's when Krishna smiled and said —

"Do your duty. Have faith. Even if you cannot see the end, fight with courage."

Krishna never told Arjuna to play it safe.

He told him to trust the process.

That's what love is — a battlefield of emotions, choices, and tests of faith.

You don't win by being careful;

You win by being courageous.

Love rewards the brave — the ones who choose to stay,

To fight for what's right, and to believe in something bigger than themselves.

Love Is Made in Heaven

They say marriages are made in heaven,

But I believe love itself is made in heaven.

Every time something new begins — a relationship, a job, a dream —

It's like giving birth to a new life.

It's fragile, innocent, and needs care.

When two people fall in love, something sacred is born —

a relationship that didn't exist before.

It's your shared energy.

Your baby.

Would a parent give up on their child because it got sick once?

No. They'd protect it, heal it, and do everything to make it safe again.

Love deserves the same.

You can't just throw it away because something feels uncertain.

You nurture it, feed it trust, protect it with patience, and keep it safe from negativity.

When you treat love with that kind of reverence,

the universe rewards you —

because God always supports those who protect what He has blessed them with.

But most of us don't live like that anymore.

We fear our image.

Since childhood, our parents have told us to be "good," to be "obedient," and not to "disappoint others."

We grow up trying to be perfect — the good child, the good friend, the good partner.

And the moment we choose something that contradicts that image, we panic.

We fear that people will no longer see us the same way.

This fear of breaking an image is one of the biggest cages we live in.

No one's life is perfect.

It's impossible to make everyone happy.

But most of our suffering comes not from what *happened*,

But from what we *imagined could happen*.

We cry over stories that never even existed —

the "what ifs," the "maybes," the "what will they think?"

And that's where trust dies —

in the space between what's real and what we imagine.

Not Everything Is About You

I once had a close friend who told me,

"If I marry someone from another caste, my family will disown me."

He truly believed that.

And I remember thinking — this is not fear of losing family; this is fear of *disappointing their image of you*.

But here's something I've come to realise —

Not every problem in your life is about *you*.

Sometimes, you are just the channel through which others are meant to learn their lessons.

Maybe your love story is meant to open your parents' hearts.

Maybe your courage is what changes their beliefs.

Maybe your experience is the one that breaks a pattern for the generations to come.

So when you face resistance, don't think, *"Why is this happening to me?"*

Think, *"Maybe this is happening through me."*

Because God doesn't make mistakes.

He doesn't randomly connect two souls.

If two people from different backgrounds fall in love, it's not rebellion — it's divine design.

The story of Sati and Shiva is the purest example of divine commitment.

Sati Devi, the daughter of King Daksha, was born into royalty.

Her father wanted her to marry a rich king,

Someone who matched their caste, status, and family name.

But Sati's heart was already devoted to Lord Shiva —

The ascetic who lived among ashes, covered in sacred dust,

Who cared nothing for riches or society.

To her father, Shiva looked unworthy.

To Sati, he was everything divine.

Despite her father's anger and society's disapproval,

She married Shiva, following her soul's truth.

Later, when her father insulted Shiva in front of everyone,

Sati couldn't bear it.

She gave up her life in the fire —

Not out of weakness, but out of sacred love.

And that wasn't the end.

Shiva, heartbroken but unwavering, waited for her return.

Sati was reborn as Parvati — and they reunited.

That is the power of love and commitment.

The kind that transcends time, death, and lifetimes.

The Eternal Energy of Love

When we pray to Shiva and Parvati,

We're not just praying to gods.

We're praying to the first love story of the universe —

A love so powerful it created the energy that holds everything together.

Even Hanuman, the greatest devotee,

was born with the grace of Shiva himself —

Sent to earth for one purpose:

To unite Lord Rama and Sita.

Think about it —

Even divine beings take form to reunite love.

So when your love is pure,

When your intentions are clean,

And when your heart beats with faith instead of fear —

The universe *has* to support you.

Because love is not just a feeling —

It's divine energy.

When you stand firm in your love,

with trust, faith, and confidence,

You're walking on the same path that gods once walked.

Love doesn't ask you to play safe.

It asks you to trust the unknown —

To take one step forward even when you can't see the next.

Because that's what faith is.

It's not knowing the whole path —

It's believing the path will appear when you start walking.

And when you walk with that kind of faith,

You'll see the universe walk with you —

Guiding, protecting, and rewarding you every step of the way.

When Parvati decided she wanted to marry Shiva, she didn't play it safe.

She didn't doubt.

She trusted her love so profoundly that the entire universe had to align with her.

And that's what true trust is —

a devotion so strong that the divine itself has no option but to stand by you.

All the gods we pray to today — Rama, Sita, Krishna, Radha, Parvati, Shiva

They all taught us one thing through their stories:

Stand by your truth.

Fight for what you love.

Trust what your soul knows.

If you keep playing it safe,

you'll never live the life meant for you.

When you play safe, you say to the universe,

"I don't trust you."

And the universe mirrors that right back —

It stops trusting you with miracles.

Because miracles require courage.

Faith is when you jump before you see the net.

And trust is believing that the net will appear.

The more you play it safe,

the smaller your life becomes.

You shrink your dreams to fit your fears.

You dim your light to make others comfortable.

But that's not what you were born for.

You were born to live — fully, fearlessly, and freely.

Chapter 7

THE FRIEND WHO FELT LIKE LIGHT

Life was not easy.

In fact, it felt like I was walking through darkness with no idea where the path led.

The days didn't feel like days anymore — they were just long stretches of time I had to survive.

Every sunrise felt heavier than the last.

I'd wake up hoping to feel better, but grief had its own stubborn rhythm.

There were days when I didn't even have the energy to speak.

Nights when I stared at the ceiling until morning.

The silence around me was so loud that even my own heartbeat started to sound like noise.

I was exhausted — not just mentally, but spiritually.

I had forgotten what peace felt like.

And then, one ordinary day, something extraordinary happened.

The Universe Sent Karthik

And then, in the middle of all that darkness, someone familiar walked into my life — not new, not unknown, just *unnoticed until then.*

His name was **Karthik**.

He was always there — part of my larger circle of friends — someone I had exchanged polite hellos with, maybe shared a few jokes, but never anything deep.

He was the kind of person who always had a calm, peaceful energy.

He wasn't loud or attention-seeking.

He had a certain stillness about him — the kind that made you feel comfortable even without words.

I had always felt that peaceful vibe from him, even before we were close.

But at that time, I never paid much attention to it.

He was just "that nice person" everyone liked to have around.

Little did I know that same calmness would one day become the anchor that pulled me out of a storm.

I still remember the first few conversations.

They weren't intense or emotional.

They were just… simple.

He asked me how I was doing — not in the casual way people ask, but like he genuinely wanted to know.

He listened, really listened.

Not once did he interrupt or rush to give advice.

He just sat there, present, patient, steady.

And something about that steadiness started to calm the storm inside me.

My Answered Prayer

Looking back now, I realise — Karthik was my *answered prayer.*

I didn't ask the universe for a new person.

I asked for strength.

I asked for peace.

I asked to be reminded that I was still worth something.

And instead of sending those things directly,

the universe sent Karthik.

He didn't come into my life to love me —

He came to show me how to love *myself* again.

For the first time in a long time, I didn't feel like I was drowning.

He didn't try to fix me, but his presence itself started to mend what was broken.

It was like standing in sunlight after months of rain —

You don't even realise how much you missed the warmth until it touches your skin again.

I often say this — **Karthik was another form of Krishna for me.**

Not because he performed miracles,

but because he made me remember the divinity within myself.

He gave me strength when I couldn't find any.

He brought courage into my conversations.

He taught me that healing doesn't always come in the form of romance — sometimes it comes in the form of presence.

Peace Has a Face

I can't explain it, but being around Karthik felt *safe.*

There were no pretences, no expectations, no drama.

Just calm.

When I spoke, he didn't rush to respond — he absorbed my words as they mattered. And for the first time, I felt heard.

Truly heard.

He never said things like *"Don't cry"* or *"You'll get over it."*

He allowed me to cry.

He gave me space to fall apart — and somehow, I started putting myself back together again in that space.

With him, there were no big promises.

But there was consistency.

A quiet reassurance that he would be there.

I didn't have to ask.

I just knew.

And for someone who had been left without explanation,

That silent kind of assurance felt divine.

When Healing Begins Without You Realising

Healing doesn't start with big decisions.

It starts with small, quiet moments — the kind you don't even notice until much later.

For me, it began when Karthik said something simple yet powerful:

"If I can believe in your strength, why can't you?"

That one line made me stop in my tracks.

It was like someone had just held a mirror to me — showing me a version of myself that I had completely forgotten existed.

If someone else could see potential in me when I felt like a complete failure,

Maybe I wasn't broken after all.

Maybe I had just lost sight of who I truly was.

That day, I made a silent promise to myself —

to stop trying to fix everything around me

and start understanding what was happening within me.

And that's when I realised something profound —

The purest form of love is not grand gestures, long conversations, or constant reassurance.

It's when someone creates a space where you feel safe to be your most authentic self.

Where you can cry without embarrassment.

Where you can vent without fear of judgment.

Where you can speak and someone gently asks —

"Do you want advice, or do you just want me to listen?"

That's what Karthik gave me.

He never rushed me to "move on."

He never dismissed my feelings or tried to solve them like a problem.

He simply offered me space —

a space where I could be vulnerable and still feel safe.

Feeling safe — emotionally, mentally, and physically — is the foundation of every healthy relationship.

It's the invisible thread that holds everything together.

Without it, even love can't survive.

You can have passion, attraction, laughter, and shared dreams,

but if you don't feel safe — if you can't trust that your heart is protected

then none of the other things matter.

Safety is what lets you breathe.

It's what lets you open up, communicate, and grow.

It's what gives you the courage to be honest — not just with others, but with yourself.

Most people think relationships are built on love.

But love alone isn't enough.

Love may ignite the connection,

but safety keeps the flame alive.

Because when you feel safe,

you stop performing and start existing.

You stop trying to be perfect and allow yourself to be human.

And that's when real intimacy begins —

not from trying harder,

but from finally feeling that you don't have to try at all.

That's what my friendship with Karthik was built on —

safety.

He gave me the gift of stillness in a time of chaos.

And that stillness became the foundation on which I rebuilt myself.

I learned that no amount of attraction or admiration can replace the peace that comes from simply feeling safe in someone's presence.

And when you find that kind of connection — even once — you understand what love in its truest form really feels like.

The Change Was Subtle

After meeting Karthik, something inside me began to shift.

Not loudly. Not like a sudden realisation.

It was slow, quiet — like the way dawn creeps in after a long, dark night.

I didn't wake up one morning.

I didn't suddenly stop crying or stop thinking about my past.

But I started to feel small changes.

Tiny, almost invisible ones.

I became calmer.

I spoke less, but with more meaning.

My reactions softened.

The heaviness in my thoughts started to fade, just a little.

For months, I had lived like a wound — open, raw, and restless.

Everything hurts. Every small thing felt like a trigger.

But now, I am beginning to feel human again.

Not "fine," not "fixed," but human.

And no, this wasn't love.

Not the kind we usually talk about — the kind with butterflies, fireworks, or promises.

This was different.

It was *adoration.*

A soul-level gratitude for someone who came into my life without expectation,

and stayed without any reason.

There was no drama between us, no confessions, no games.

Just peace.

And after everything I'd been through, peace felt like magic.

Our energies matched naturally.

He never tried too hard, and neither did I.

We didn't have to fill the silence.

Sometimes we just sat — two people with unspoken stories, quietly healing in each other's presence.

I started sleeping better.

Started eating again — real meals, not just coffee and biscuits.

I started waking up with fewer "what ifs."

Life still wasn't perfect,

but for the first time, it was peaceful.

And peace, I realised, was everything I had ever wanted.

The Decision to Begin Again

One evening, I was sitting on my bed, looking at an old picture of myself

a photo from before all the chaos began.

I looked happy there. Genuinely happy.

But I could also see something else - innocence.

A girl who didn't know how strong she could be until life tested her.

That night, I decided to rebuild myself.

I took that photo and kept it on my mirror.

Below it, I wrote all the qualities the new version of me would have.

Confident. Peaceful.

Mature. Composed.

A person who responds, not reacts.

Someone who listens more and overthinks less.

Calm. Grounded.

Gentle, but strong.

Less dependent. More centred.

Full of love, but not desperate for it.

More passionate. More alive.

I wanted to become *her.*

And for the first time, I wasn't just wishing —

I was choosing.

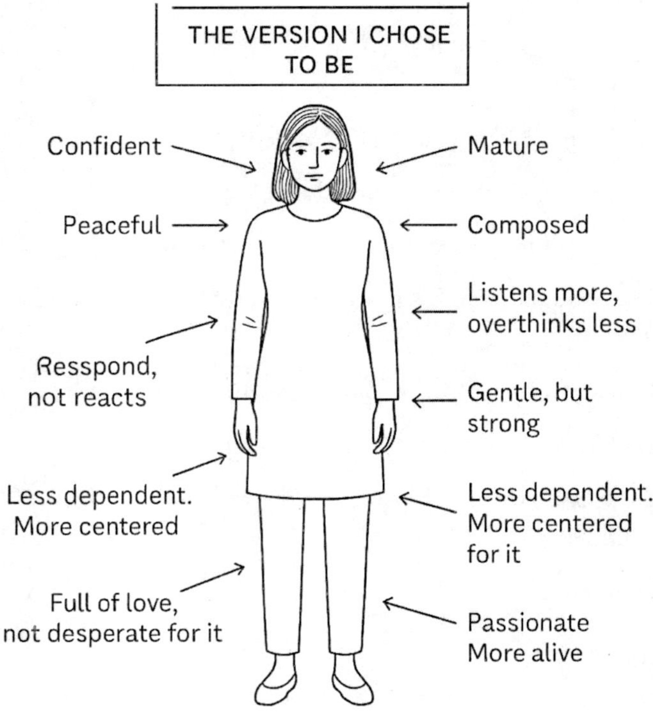

The Death of the Old Self

But here's what no one tells you —

To become a new person, your old self has to die.

Not literally, of course.

But the parts of you that are built on fear, insecurity, and past pain —

They can't come along into your next chapter.

You can't be the same person and expect life to change.

You can't keep the same beliefs and expect new experiences.

It doesn't work that way.

I realised I'd been holding onto too much —

old arguments, old fears, old labels.

I wanted peace, but I was still feeding the patterns that caused chaos.

So I began letting go, piece by piece.

Some days it felt freeing.

Other days, it felt like a loss.

Because when you outgrow your pain,

you also outgrow the version of yourself who learned to survive it.

And that's hard.

There were nights I felt like giving up.

I cried, I questioned, I doubted everything — even myself.

But one thing I told myself every single time was —

"No one else will face the consequences of your inaction."

If I didn't change, nothing else would.

If I didn't move, I'd keep living the same story on loop.

And I didn't want that anymore.

What Karthik Taught Me

So I started watching Karthik closely — not as a habit, but as inspiration.

He had something I wanted — not his life, but his energy.

He was passionate about everything he did.

Even the most minor things — like fixing his desk, helping a friend, or making plans —

He did them with full attention.

He didn't rush.

He didn't complain.

He just showed up.

The way he gave 100% to everything — work, people, even his rest —

It was inspiring.

He reminded me that passion isn't loud or dramatic.

It's consistent.

It's the quiet discipline of giving your best — even when no one's watching.

That's when I realised —

I didn't have to chase a "new life."

I just had to show up differently in the one I already had.

I decided to become more passionate, more patient, more intentional —

to live as if every small thing mattered.

Because it does.

The Slow Rebuild

Becoming a new person isn't easy.

It's not like changing clothes or cutting your hair.

It's uncomfortable. It's messy.

It's like tearing down an old house while still living in it.

Some days, I felt proud of how far I'd come.

Other days, I felt like I hadn't moved an inch.

Healing is like that — it doesn't move in a straight line.

But I kept going.

I started small — waking up early, reading again, journaling.

I began making routines that nourished me rather than drained me.

I spoke kindly to myself.

Even when I failed, I reminded myself: *You're learning.*

And every time I fell back into my old patterns,

I chose to rise again — not stronger, but wiser.

Slowly, the girl who once doubted everything

started trusting again.

The girl who thought her life ended
started dreaming again.
And the girl who believed she was broken
started believing she was whole.
All of this happened because one person —
without asking for anything in return —
showed me what safety, kindness, and belief felt like.
Karthik didn't heal me.
He simply reminded me that I could heal myself.
And that realisation changed everything.
I'm not the same person I was when this story began.
And I'm grateful for that.
Because the person I am now —
She feels deeply, but she doesn't beg for love.
She gives, but she knows when to step back.
She believes, but she doesn't chase.
She loves, but never loses herself.
I don't thank Karthik just for being there —
I thank him for reminding me that peace can exist,
and that healing isn't something you find.
It's something you *build*, one day at a time.

The Magic of Divine Timing

It still amazes me how he entered my life exactly when I needed him.

Not a day earlier, not a day later.

I often think of how the universe works —

how people are sent into your story like chapters you didn't plan to write,

But I can't imagine the book without it.

That's what Karthik became —

a chapter that healed me, guided me, and reminded me of my worth.

He wasn't my destiny — He was my direction.

He didn't promise forever,

but he showed me what *presence* feels like.

He showed me that love can exist without expectations.

As my days grew lighter, I realised something —

He wasn't the reason I healed; he was the mirror that showed me *how.*

When someone sees you in your lowest and still reminds you of your light,

you start seeing it too. That's what Karthik did for me.

He reflected to me the version of myself that I thought had died.

I began to take small steps again —

reading, learning, setting goals.

I applied to universities not out of desperation, but out of determination.

I wanted to live again.

He never once said *"forget your past."*

He said, *"Remember who you are."*

And that changed everything.

He is my Anchor

Karthik stood like an anchor —

not to hold me down, but to keep me steady while I found my own balance.

He watched me rise slowly,

from someone who thought life was over

to someone who started dreaming again.

When I cried, he didn't ask me to stop.

When I smiled, he celebrated quietly.

And when I doubted myself, he reminded me —

"You've already survived your worst days. The rest is just living."

Those words still echo in my mind.

A Different Kind of Love

It's funny how people define relationships.

For me, Karthik wasn't a love story — he was a *life story.*

He never tried to replace what I lost.

He helped me rebuild what I had forgotten — *myself.*

It wasn't about romance.

It was about resonance.

We matched vibrations — peace for peace, presence for presence.

And in that space, I learned that love isn't always about *being together.*

Sometimes, it's about *helping each other remember who you are.*

Even now, when I think of Karthik, I smile.

I don't call him "the one who helped me get away" —

I call him *the one who helped me stay.*

He reminded me that the universe never leaves you stranded.

It always sends help —

sometimes through people, sometimes through pain.

I still didn't heal completely then,

but his presence became the reality check I needed —

to see where I was still hurting

and where I needed to grow.

He didn't carry my pain for me,

But he made sure I didn't carry it alone.

A Thank You That Words Can't Hold

There are some people you can never thank enough —

because their presence itself was the miracle.

Karthik was that person for me.

The strength he gave me,

the courage he reminded me of,

the peace he helped me rebuild —

They are things I carry with me every day.

I can confidently say now:

I didn't survive my heartbreak *alone.*

The universe sent help —

And it came in the form of a friend named Karthik.

The Woman I Became While Waiting for No One

When I met Karthik,

I didn't ask how long this would last.

I didn't try to name what it was.

All I knew was that being around him felt peaceful.

But I also knew something else —

I was better, not completely healed.

I was stronger than before, yes,

but still a work in progress.

I could see that even Karthik carried many of the same fears Arjun once did.

And that awareness made me pause.

I told myself quietly, firmly —

I do not want to be affected by another person again.

I do not want to wait for anyone again in life.

And the truth?

The feelings I felt for Karthik were not as intense

as what I once felt for Arjun in the beginning.

But this was different.

Softer.

Calmer.

More stable than infatuation, yet more than friendship.

He never made promises,

but his presence was steady.

He made me feel safe.

And safety — I've learned —

It is one of the rarest, purest forms of love.

There was calm.

There was pain, yes — healing isn't painless —

But there was also a quiet confidence I'd never felt before.

The kind that whispers,

"Even if I walk alone, I'll be okay."

Because real love doesn't always arrive as romance.

Sometimes, it comes as a friend,

a guide,

a mirror, reminding you who you are.

And if this was meant to unfold into something more, it would.

If not, we would simply remain friends.

That was the peace I held in my heart.

Somewhere along this journey, I remembered a story —

The story of Sati and Shiva.

Sati didn't chase Shiva.

She didn't beg, plead, or fast to *get* him.

She meditated to become Shakti —

her divine, whole self.

She aligned with her own energy.

She didn't ask, "Will he choose me?"

She rested in the truth that their union already existed in spirit.

That's why her aura became magnetic.

And in that moment, I understood something life-changing —

for me to truly get what I want in life,

I must become someone it is hard to walk away from.

Not because I demand.

Not because I control.

But because my energy, my peace, my wholeness

naturally holds space for everything meant for me.

Desperation is born from fear —

fear of loss, fear of lack, fear of time.

But true power, true love, comes from wholeness.

From knowing: *I am complete.*

That is the energy I chose to live by.

I no longer wanted a love that demanded I shrink, adjust, or lose myself.

I no longer wished to beg for understanding

or settle for half-efforts dressed as love.

I wanted someone who would take a stand for me

the way I would take a stand for them —

even when the path became difficult.

When I decided to go to Europe for my master's,

I knew things would change.

I wouldn't see Karthik the same way anymore.

But for the first time in years, I wasn't scared.

I didn't ask,

"What if he forgets me?"

or

"What if this ends?"

Because I had built something stronger than attachment —

faith.

Faith that what is meant for me will never leave me.

Faith that those meant to stay, will.

And faith that even if they don't,

Life will always refill the spaces they once occupied.

That's when I realised the truth:

I didn't want to be loved because someone stayed.

I wanted to be loved because my energy made them want to.

And the only way to do that

was to become a woman so whole within herself

that love could only **add** to her peace — not replace it.

So I began rebuilding myself from the inside out.

Piece by piece.

Habit by habit.

Belief by belief.

I stopped asking for timelines.

I stopped demanding closure.

I stopped chasing healing —

I simply lived it.

There was once a time when distance terrified me.

But now, I welcome it.

Because sometimes, distance isn't separation —

It is an expansion.

It is the universe saying,

"You've learned what you need here. Now grow."

And that's exactly what I did.

I grew.

I learned to let things unfold without resistance.

I learned that people who leave often create space for better energy to enter.

And I learned that love, when it is real, doesn't need to be held tightly —

it flows freely and fearlessly.

Now, when I look back,

I see I didn't lose anyone.

I found myself.

And that is the most divine love story I could have ever asked for —

the woman I became

while waiting for no one.

Chapter 8

WHEN SOUMYA MET MANASA

When I went to Europe, I thought healing would come from distance.

Not because I wanted to run away —

But because I believed new places could give me a new life.

I thought maybe a new country, new streets, new people, and a new routine would help me breathe differently.

I believed that changing my surroundings would change the way my heart felt.

But when I actually reached there, Europe looked nothing like the life I had lived so far.

Everything was new.

Everything was different.

Everything felt like a story I had never read before.

My room was the first surprise.

In India, I was used to adjusting — one object for multiple things, one corner used for everything.

But here, everything had a separate object, a separate purpose, a separate place.

There was a basket only for towels.

A stand only for shoes.

A hook only for coats.

A small drawer only for keys.

Even a soft cloth only for cleaning glasses.

It felt funny at first — like, why do they have a thing for everything?

But slowly, I understood… this is how they live.

Organised.

Peaceful.

Structured.

Simple.

The floors were different, too —

In India, you always feel the ground under your feet, the cool tiles, the sound of walking.

But in Europe, there were thick mats everywhere.

No sound.

No echo.

Just soft steps.

It almost felt like walking in quietness.

And my bed —

Oh, my princess bed.

White sheets, fluffy pillows, a soft comforter that swallowed me whole when I slept.

For the first time in months, I slept without crying.

The bed may have healed me a little, too.

Every morning, my neighbour auntie used to bake something.

Bread… Muffins… cinnamon rolls… cookies.

And that warm, sweet smell used to drift straight into my room.

I didn't even know her properly, but she smiled every time she saw me.

Sometimes she said, "Bonjour!"

Sometimes, "Good morning!"

And sometimes just a smile that felt like a hug.

But English became difficult.

Not because I didn't know it — I did —

But because their accent, their speed, and their expressions felt so different.

Sometimes I just nodded and prayed I understood correctly.

Sometimes I laughed at myself after coming home.

Just 100 meters away from my house, there was a beautiful park.

Small, but full of life.

Surrounded by tall trees that looked golden during sunset.

A walking path that looked like something out of a movie.

Benches where people sat with books, coffee, or just silence.

I saw people from all age groups there —

Children running freely,

Teenagers laughing loudly,

Young couples sitting together,

Older adults taking slow walks,

Mothers with prams,

Fathers chasing their kids,

Pet owners with dogs that looked happier than humans.

Some came for fitness — yes.

But most came for something else —

Just to live that moment.

To breathe.

To sit.

To enjoy the sky.

To be present.

Nobody was rushing.

Nobody was judging.

Nobody was comparing.

Everyone was minding their own work, their own peace, their own world.

And suddenly the world felt different to me, too.

Their dressing was different as well.

Simple yet elegant.

Warm coats, long scarves, and boots that made every outfit look stylish.

People didn't dress to impress others —

They dress to feel comfortable in their own skin.

And one thing I always noticed —

their gates.

Big, beautiful gates for every house.

Sometimes black,

sometimes golden,

sometimes wooden,

but always tall and grand —

as if every house had its own personality.

Living there felt like stepping into a different universe.

One where life moved slowly,

people lived softly,

and happiness came from small things —

like warm bread, quiet parks, fresh air, and soft mornings.

It made me question everything I knew about life till then.

When I finally joined college in Europe, everything felt unreal.

The campus looked nothing like the Indian colleges I grew up seeing.

The first day itself felt like stepping onto a movie set.

The buildings were tall but simple — white walls, wide glass windows, wooden doors with silver handles.

Every corridor smelled like a mix of fresh paper, coffee, and winter air.

The floors were so clean that my footsteps felt too loud, as if I was walking inside a library.

The classrooms were even more different.

No wooden benches, no noisy fans, no broken desks.

Just soft chairs arranged in a curve, huge digital screens, clean whiteboards, and long tables where everyone had their own space.

There were charging points everywhere.

Even under the tables.

I felt like such a foreigner — both in the room and within myself.

The professors were calm… too calm.

No shouting, no rushing, no calling out roll numbers loudly.

They spoke slowly, with smiles, as if every student deserved time to understand.

They asked questions like they genuinely wanted to hear our thoughts, not like they were waiting to catch us off guard.

The cafés on campus were warm and cosy.

Soft lights, the smell of baked croissants, people sipping coffee from mugs instead of paper cups, and a soft hum of conversations in different accents.

Sometimes I would just sit there and observe.

People from 20+ countries.

Different cultures.

Different languages.

Different energies.

Everyone minding their own work, but somehow together.

Some students looked effortlessly stylish —

long coats, messy buns, small gold hoops, black boots.

Some students carried huge laptops and spoke in perfect, fluent English with confidence I envied.

Some looked like they were born for these spaces.

And then there was me — holding onto my books, my scarf, and my fears, all at the same time.

Everywhere I looked, life felt new.

New faces.

New systems.

New routines.

New ways of learning.

New ways of talking.

New ways of living.

And yet, inside me…

the same old emptiness.

The same old ache.

The same old fear of being alone.

The same whisper of heartbreak that hadn't left me, even after crossing continents.

One day, I entered my classroom — stressed, tired, and absent-minded — and something unexpected happened.

There she was.

Manasa.

Sitting casually in the second row.

Hair tied, wearing a simple sweater, scrolling on her phone like the entire universe wasn't shifting for me at that moment.

I froze.

Of all the people I expected to see in a European classroom, she was the last.

It felt like seeing a familiar song in a foreign playlist.

My heart didn't know whether to feel shocked, relieved, or confused.

Back in India, she was Arjun's friend.

A familiar face, yes.

But not someone close to my heart.

Not someone I ever imagined would walk into my life again — especially not on another continent.

But there she was — real, present, smiling in the same soft way she always did.

I walked up to her hesitantly, unsure if she would even recognise me.

And the moment she saw me, her eyes lit up.

"Soumya? You're here?" she said, as if life had planned this meeting beautifully behind our backs.

I felt something inside me soften for the first time in months.

It felt like the universe was telling me,

"You're not alone."

We didn't become close immediately.

There was no dramatic hug, no emotional scene.

Just two girls, sitting beside each other, quietly sharing the same space after years —

in a country neither of us belonged to.

But something shifted that day.

Something opened.

Something calmed.

Little did I know —

Throughout my healing process, it wasn't strangers who healed me.

Not new faces.

Not fresh beginnings with unfamiliar people.

It came through people I *already* knew.

Through conversations I never planned.

Through support I never expected.

I believed changing countries, changing air, changing roads would somehow silence the noise inside my heart.

But I didn't realise something important:

Pain doesn't understand geography.

It travels with you in your suitcase.

It sits beside you quietly on flights.

It unpacks itself in your new room even before you hang your curtains.

Europe was calm, beautiful, comforting —

But inside, I was still shattered.

And that's when Manasa slowly walked into my life.

Not as Arjun's friend.

Not as a part of my past.

Not as someone tied to old memories.

In Europe, she became just… Manasa.

And that made everything different.

We started talking naturally —

about classes, food cravings, cultural shocks, assignments, weather, random silly things.

But behind those small talks, something deeper was happening.

There was calm around her.

A steady, soft kind of calm that your heart leans into.

Not excitement.

Not drama.

Just stillness.

And I needed that more than anything.

She never demanded my story.

She never forced me to open up.

She never asked questions that felt heavy.

She just stayed close… quietly.

Sometimes the greatest healing doesn't come from people who talk loudly

but from someone who simply sits beside you without asking you to be okay.

During this time, I was trying to rebuild myself — painfully, slowly, and awkwardly.

I had joined an MBA programme, something completely different from my original background.

Every class felt like a challenge.

Every assignment felt like I was pretending to understand.

But I wanted change, even if I wasn't ready for it yet.

And somewhere in the middle of this chaos, Manasa existed —

not as *Arjun's friend* anymore,

but as just… **Manasa.**

She lived a few houses away from me in the student accommodation.

That alone felt like a soft reassurance.

Like the universe had given me a familiar heartbeat in a foreign world.

It happened on a random weekday morning.

Not planned, not dramatic — just very normal.

We were sitting in the university café between two classes.

I was eating a dry croissant that tasted nothing like home,

and she was complaining that the coffee here tastes like "hot water pretending to be espresso."

For a moment, we sat in comfortable silence.

Then I randomly said,

"Manasa… the aunties in my building always bake. Every day, my corridor smells like vanilla and butter. I feel like learning something."

She didn't even take a second.

She looked at me and said,

"Bro, even I wanted to learn baking. Let's join."

Just like that.

So casually.

So easily.

As if the universe spoke through her.

And the funny thing?

That one simple "let's join" felt like healing.

Because she didn't hesitate to sit with me.

She didn't hesitate to spend time with me.

She didn't hesitate just because of "who I once was in someone's story."

Her yes made me feel human again.

After college, we walked to a cute little store near the tram stop.

It had fairy lights on the door, and baking tools hung like art on the walls.

We picked aprons like two excited children.

Mine was cream-coloured, with dusty-pink borders.

Hers was a soft lavender shade.

We both got our names embroidered on top —

Soumya and *Manasa* —

in tiny cursive gold thread.

We left the shop laughing, holding the aprons like they were some achievement.

It was silly.

But it meant something.

Because for the first time in months, I felt like I was doing something just for myself.

We dressed up intentionally for the first day of baking class —

not for anyone else,

but because we both wanted to feel alive in a new way.

I wore a light beige sweater tucked into my jeans and white sneakers.

Manasa wore this oversized pastel-blue sweatshirt and black tights with ankle boots.

The European cold breeze hit our faces as we walked.

The street lights were golden.

The sky was already turning violet.

And everything suddenly looked cinematic.

We giggled while walking. She pushed me when I stopped to tie my shoe,

I teased her for walking too slowly.

It felt like a movie scene where two girls were trying to find their way back to themselves.

The moment we entered, it felt magical.

Soft yellow lights.

White counters lined with bowls and whisks.

Shelves stacked with sprinkles, moulds, trays, cocoa powder jars, and tiny pastel-colored spoons.

The room smelled like chocolate and cinnamon.

Our instructor — a lady in her 40s with short brown hair — wore a mustard cardigan with flour stains near the elbow.

She greeted everyone with a warm *"Bonjour, girls!"*

People from all over the world were there —

a Spanish girl with red lipstick,

two Italian boys who joked even while whisking,

a French woman who baked like a professional.

We baked a simple vanilla sponge cake.

We cracked eggs wrong.

We spilled sugar everywhere.

We whisked too fast and splashed batter on our aprons.

We shouted at each other for ruining the mixture and then laughed immediately.

And the entire studio smelled like warm cake.

In that moment —

for the first time in a very long time — I didn't miss anyone.

Not my past.

Not my pain.

Not even the people I thought my life depended on.

I felt present.

Alive.

New.

We walked home smiling.

Not loudly.

Not dramatically.

Just that soft kind of smile that comes when your soul feels a little lighter.

Later that night, I spoke to Karthik —

a short, simple, grounding conversation, the kind that doesn't take space but somehow fills your heart.

Karthik and I never talked every day.

Our conversations were rare.

But whenever we did talk, we shared everything —

little updates, random thoughts, tiny moments that mattered.

Some friendships are peaceful like that —

They don't demand anything,

they don't add pressure,

they feel like a warm blanket on a cold day.

That night felt different.

For the first time, out of pure excitement,

I felt like telling him something —

that I didn't miss Arjun at all that day,

even though I spent the whole evening with someone who used to be close to him.

It surprised me.

And it strangely comforted me.

Karthik told me about his day, too.

His mom had cooked Indian food —

a proper, hot, home-style meal —

And he said he ate it so happily,

"Bro, finally something that tastes like home. I didn't realise how much I missed this."

I laughed because I knew exactly what he meant.

I missed that food too.

I missed home.

But for the first time, the missing didn't hurt.

It felt warm. Familiar. Soft.

After texting Karthik,

I kept my phone aside…

And for the first time in months —

I slept.

Not because I was exhausted.

Not because I cried myself tired.

Not because my emotions burned me out.

I slept because my heart finally breathed differently.

Because something inside me loosened.

Because a small part of me finally felt alive again.

Chapter 9

HOW EUROPE BROKE ME OPEN — AND PUT ME BACK TOGETHER

When I landed in Italy, it didn't feel like I was beginning a new life.

It felt like I was pressing pause on the old one.

The airport was buzzing — wheels clicking on marble floors, people speaking in languages I didn't recognise, warm lights reflecting off glass walls. And there I was, standing with my suitcase in one hand and a restless heaviness in my chest, thinking,

"Maybe it will feel easier to breathe here."

Not because I wanted to run away.

Not because I wanted to erase the past.

I just needed a little distance —

a little space between me and what was hurting.

I thought maybe a new country could give me that.

Everything around me was unfamiliar anyway —

streets lined with rough cobblestones,

faces that had no idea who I was

or what I had been carrying inside me.

New air that smelled of fresh bread and cold wind.

New mornings, new routines, new possibilities.

For a moment, I really believed that newness alone could heal me.

But here's something no one tells you:

Your mind travels with you.

Your wounds travel with you.

And your fears find a seat next to you on the flight.

New Place doesn't reset emotions.

Healing doesn't begin when you move to a new place.

Healing begins when **you** move differently inside yourself.

I didn't know this yet.

I was about to learn it — slowly, painfully, beautifully — in ways I never expected.

Italy was nothing like home.

The moment I stepped outside the airport, the air felt different — lighter, colder, smelling faintly of roasted chestnuts and bakery bread.

Even the sounds felt different: heels clicking on cobblestones, the soft hum of bicycles, church bells in the distance, people speaking Italian with a musical rhythm.

I remember thinking:

"This Place feels like a movie. So why does my heart still feel so heavy?"

But life doesn't slow down just because you're healing.

And Italy, as beautiful as it was, was an expensive dream.

Two Broke Girls in their part-time jobs

It didn't take us long to realise:

We needed part-time jobs.

Not as an option —

but for survival.

Manasa and I had some money coming from home, but barely enough to pay rent, groceries, transport, and the occasional treat. Living abroad teaches you something quickly:

You learn the value of every euro.

And the value of every choice.

So we began the hunt.

The job hunt in Italy deserves its own movie.

Manasa and I walked into cafés with our timid smiles,

printed CVs,

Google-translated Italian phrases,

and all the enthusiasm two broke girls could squeeze into themselves.

"Ciao… abbiamo, um… bisogno di lavoro… part-time?"

(We were definitely not fluent.)

Most café owners smiled politely.

Some laughed gently.

Some nodded sympathetically.

Most said no.

Some said, "Maybe next week."

A few didn't understand us at all.

But every rejection felt manageable

because we were together.

We would walk out of each café, look at each other, roll our eyes,

and burst out laughing.

That laughter was our coping mechanism.

It kept us alive.

Finally — The Café That Became Our Second Home

One chilly evening, after walking nearly 8,000 steps across the old town,

We entered a small café tucked between two old stone buildings.

It smelled heavenly — like a mix of espresso, cinnamon, and freshly baked croissants.

The owner, an older man with kind eyes, looked at our CVs, looked at us, and said:

"Okay. Try tomorrow. Evening shift."

Just like that.

No dramatic music.

No fate written in stars.

Just a simple yes.

The next day, we wore our simplest clothes —

jeans, sweaters, jackets —

tied our hair,

and walked to the café with nervous excitement.

We weren't baristas yet,

But that's what we became — slowly, clumsily, beautifully.

Life Became a Rhythm

Our days started blending into each other:

Morning — College

Running through cobblestone paths, climbing steep stairs, and walking into classrooms filled with students from all over the world.

Afternoon — Assignments

Sitting in the university café, scribbling notes, whispering jokes, planning our part-time shifts.

Evening — Part-time Café

Our aprons tied tightly, hair pinned back, steaming milk, burning fingers, repeating orders loudly, smiling at strangers, learning how to be useful in a foreign world.

Night — Contemplating life

Walking home under orange street lamps, sharing snacks, sitting by the river, talking about life and heartbreaks and dreams… until silence felt enough.

We became a unit.

Two girls trying to survive.

Two girls trying to grow.

Two girls learning how to exist again.

The Café — My Therapy in Disguise

The café became a chapter in my healing story.

The warm smell of coffee,

the way the machines hissed,

the clinking sound of ceramic cups,

the soft Italian music playing in the background —

All of it felt grounding.

Customers were kind.

Some asked where we were from.

Some taught us Italian phrases.

A few even complimented our improving milk foam.

Working there made me forget my pain in small doses.

Pain didn't leave.

It just rested during the shift.

As if it was saying,

"I'll wait. You can take this tiny break."

Manasa was always around.

In class.

In the café.

During our daily walks.

Buying groceries together.

Laughing at our empty wallets.

Sharing one coffee like queens.

We lived like two broke girls,

but we lived like we owned the city.

€2 pastries tasted like luxury.

Sitting on cold benches felt like therapy.

Walking by the river at night felt like healing.

People talk about romantic soulmates.

But sometimes a friend becomes your soul's nurse.

The Gym — The First Real Step Toward the New Me

After our evening shift, Manasa would usually head back home.

I went the other way.

I turned left, toward the gym.

Joining a gym wasn't new to me.

But this time, my reason was.

The gym in Italy felt unfamiliar in a strange way —

too clean, too quiet, too organised.

Bright lights.

Clear mirrors.

Machines I didn't even recognise.

Weights neatly arranged by colour.

Soft music playing in the background.

No crowd.

No noise.

No rush.

Just space.

Just effort.

Just me.

On the first day, I stood in front of the mirror with two small pink dumbbells in my hands and said to myself, quietly but firmly,

"This time, I'm staying."

And for the first time, I believed in myself.

Why This Time Was Different

All my previous gym attempts had followed a pattern:

Start → Get excited → Miss 2 days → Lose motivation → Quit → Feel guilty

But this time, I wanted to understand *why*.

So one night, I took out my notebook — the pastel blue one —

and wrote down all the limiting beliefs I had about fitness:

– "I always fail."

– "My body doesn't change."

– "I can't stay consistent."

– "Maybe fitness is not for me."

– "Every time I try, something goes wrong."

Then I asked myself:

"Where did all this begin?"

I realised:

My thoughts were negative.

My feelings were defeated.

My actions were inconsistent.

My beliefs were weak.

Everything was out of alignment.

My Beliefs: *"I want to lose weight."*

My Thoughts: *"What's the point?"*

My Feelings: *"I'm tired."*

My Actions: *Skipping gym.*

Of course, I wasn't progressing.

The universe had no clarity on what I wanted.

So I wrote this line in big letters and stuck it on my wall:

"No one else except me pays the price for my inaction."

That sentence built discipline in me.

Even when I didn't want to go

—even when I was tired from class, café, or life—

I went.

Because I knew:

If I didn't show up, no one else would face the consequences except me.

My Routine — Discipline Becoming Identity

Gym at 6.

Walk home at 7.

Warm shower.

Simple dinner — pasta, salad, or soup.

Lavender candle on my desk.

Pink mug with warm tea.

My cute pastel journals lined up neatly.

Soft fairy lights around my window.

The faint smell of bread from the neighbour aunties.

Occasional laughter from the corridor.

My room felt like healing.

Every night, I opened my journal and wrote:

Column 1: How did I push my limits today?

Went to gym.

Cooked instead of ordering.

Completed assignment.

Didn't overthink.

Spoke to someone new.

Column 2: Where was I out of alignment?

I got anxious.

Compared to myself.

Skipped meditation.

Thought of Arjun suddenly.

Column 3: What can I improve tomorrow?

One small step.

One better choice.

One aligned decision.

Those pages were my recovery.

Those words were my rebirth.

Even with all my routines, something still felt missing.

My body was moving.

My days were structured.

My discipline was growing.

Yet somewhere deep inside, there was a quiet restlessness — not loud enough to break me, but strong enough to remind me that I was still healing.

That evening, after my workout, I didn't feel like walking back home as I usually did.

It had rained.

My mind felt heavy.

So I took a cab.

As the car moved through the wet streets, the driver looked at me through the mirror and asked gently,

"Rough day?"

I hesitated for a second and then said,

"Not just today… I'm confused about life. I'm trying so hard, but I don't really know where I'm going."

He nodded slowly, as if he understood more than I had said.

Then he asked,

"Tell me one thing… if you already knew how your life would end — that everything will work out — how would you live today?"

I said,

"Of course I'd be relaxed. I wouldn't be this anxious. But no one knows the ending, right?"

He smiled and replied,

"That's where the problem is. You are waiting to see everything fall into Place before you relax. What if you relax first — because it's already going to fall into Place?"

I stayed silent.

He continued,

"If you knew for sure that your career, your relationships, your health, your life — everything would be exactly how you want it in the end… would you still be carrying this much tension in your chest right now?"

I said softly,

"No… I don't think so."

He said,

"Then why live like the ending is uncertain?

Your mind doesn't need proof. It only needs a decision."

Then he said something that stayed with me:

"The version of you who already has what she wants is not in the future.

She already exists.

Every choice you make today is either taking you closer to her…

or taking you away from her."

The cab stopped.

I paid him.

I said thank you — a little softer than usual.

He smiled again and drove away.

But the question he asked stayed.

I stood there for a moment under the streetlight, the rain still faint in the air, my gym bag on my shoulder, my thoughts suddenly louder than before — but for the first time, not chaotic.

That was when the thought entered me.

Not from my effort.

Not from my journal.

Not from discipline.

From a stranger.

From a rainy evening.

From a moment I never planned.

"If I already knew the ending… how would I act today?"

And in that moment, I understood something simple yet powerful:

Until now, I was trying to change my life by reacting to the present.

But change actually begins when you start responding from the future.

That night, I went into my room quietly.

I didn't cry.

I didn't overthink.

I just took my notebook and wrote one line in bold letters and stuck it on the wall where I could see it every morning:

"IT IS ALREADY DONE."

Below that, I wrote:

"I am the version of me who always finds her way.

I am the version of me who always grows.

There is nothing to wait for.

I am living the reality where everything is unfolding exactly as it should."

From the next day, I started with the smallest things.

Before going to the gym, I wrote:

"I come back stronger, lighter, and proud of myself."

Before meeting Manasa, I wrote:

"We laugh today. We return happy."

Before assignments:

"I finish with ease."

Before work shifts:

"I handle everything calmly."

I stopped waiting for proof.

I started living as if the proof was already written.

And slowly — without noise, without force —

My energy changed.

I stopped reacting.

I stopped panicking.

I stopped waiting.

I started *moving.*

Not because everything outside changed immediately —

But because something inside me finally did.

And the surprising part?

It actually worked.

Not in a dramatic, overnight-miracle way —

but in the quiet, undeniable way that only real change happens.

The first sign was my mornings.

Earlier, I would wake up with heaviness.

Now, I began waking up with intention.

Some days I still felt low — but I no longer stayed there.

I would tell myself,

"Move first. Let feelings follow."

And somehow… the feelings did follow.

The second sign was in my body.

At the gym, the same weights that once felt impossible

started feeling lighter.

Not because I suddenly became strong —

But because I stopped entering the room, I was already defeated.

I walked in like the person who finishes the workout,

not the one who quits halfway.

And my body responded to that belief.

The third sign was in my relationships.

I stopped waiting for people to make me feel okay.

I showed up as the version of me who was already okay.

Some conversations became softer.

Some people became kinder.

And a few naturally drifted away —

without drama, without pain.

Just alignment.

That's when it hit me deeply:

Life doesn't change when you "hope" differently.

It changes when you "move" differently.

And for the first time in a very long time,

I wasn't trying to fix my life out of fear.

I was building it out of trust.

One of the clearest proofs that this inner shift was real came through Karthik.

Earlier, whenever he took time to reply, my mind would spiral not like before, but a bit.

A hundred questions.

A hundred fears.

A hundred imagined endings.

But one evening, after this new version of me had started taking shape, something different happened.

I had texted him after my gym session — just a simple update, something ordinary.

He didn't reply for a long time.

Earlier, that silence would have eaten me alive.

I would have checked my phone every two minutes.

I would have assumed the worst.

I would have lost my peace before losing anything else.

But that day, I didn't.

I went on with my routine.

I cooked.

I journaled.

I watched the rain from my window.

I felt calm.

Much later that night, his message came:

"Sorry, I got stuck at work… but reading your message made my day."

And I remember smiling — not out of relief,

but out of stability.

For the first time, my peace didn't depend on the timing of his reply.

It came from within me.

Another day, he casually told me about a stressful situation he was dealing with.

Earlier, I would have jumped into panic for him.

I would have worried more about his problems than my own life.

But this time, I just listened.

Truly listened.

Without losing myself in it.

After the call ended, I realized something quietly powerful:

I didn't abandon myself to be there for him.

And yet, I was fully there.

That's when I knew —

This wasn't the old me loving.

This was the healing I loved.

And one night, out of nowhere, he said something that stayed with me:

"You've changed… but in a good way. You feel stronger. Calmer. Like you finally chose yourself."

I didn't tell him about all the inner work.

About the journals.

About the gym.

About the rewiring.

About the fear, I learned to sit with.

I just smiled.

Because I knew.

This was the version of me that didn't beg for love.

This was the version that **attracted it without trying**.

THE MOMENT I UNDERSTOOD WHAT TRUE LOYALTY LOOKS LIKE

There was a phase in Europe when things became… complicated in a quiet, subtle way.

Not dramatic.

Not confrontational.

Just the kind of complications that arise when human emotions, old connections, and new relationships stand together in the same room.

Some of Manasa's and Arjun's common friends — both from India and some studying with us in Italy — had started to get uncomfortable seeing us close.

Not because they hated me.

Not because they thought I was wrong.

But because people naturally lean toward the comfort of old boundaries.

In their minds, there was an unwritten rule:

"If you were his friend, you shouldn't be her friend."

"If you cared for him, you cannot care for her."

This wasn't malicious.

It was immaturity, habit, misunderstanding, and fear, all combined.

I sensed the shift.

The slight hesitations.

The quick glances.

The half-smiles.

The awkward small talk ended too quickly.

But Manasa never changed.

Not in class.

Not at the café.

Not during our long walks.

Not even when others whispered their opinions.

She showed up next to me every single day — with the same calmness, the same care, the same effortless affection.

But one particular evening became the turning point.

THE NIGHT EVERYTHING BECAME CLEAR

It was a regular Saturday evening in Italy.

We had gone grocery shopping, carrying cheap pasta packets and milk cartons in our hands.

Our long day ended with us watching a movie in her room — the lights dim, the window slightly open allowing the cool air inside, her blanket wrapped around both of us.

We were just two girls in a foreign country, trying to create a small pocket of home.

Halfway through the movie, Manasa's phone lit up.

It was a video call from her friends — the group who once knew both Arjun and me.

She answered with her usual bright energy.

"Hello Brooo!"

"Where are you?"

"What's up?"

The screen filled with familiar faces — teasing, laughing, munching something, clearly enjoying their evening.

Then, like always, someone jokingly asked:

"Manasa… why are you STILL hanging out with Arjun's ex?"

Another one laughed and added:

"Aren't you breaking some bro code?"

It wasn't rude.

It wasn't hateful.

It was the way young people asked questions without thinking about how deeply their words could cut.

I felt my stomach tighten, but I stayed quiet.

Before I could even process how to react, Manasa straightened her back, held the phone a little higher and said — in a tone so calm, so confident, so steady — that even I couldn't believe what I was hearing:

"Bro code doesn't mean this."

The entire group went silent.

She continued, her voice firm but gentle:

"When I was born, I didn't know Arjun.

I didn't know Soumya.

I met them at different times in my life."

Her words had weight.

"Arjun came into my life earlier.

Soumya came later.

Both were different timelines.

Both were different stories.

Both are different human beings."

She took a small breath.

"Whatever happened between them is THEIR personal story.

Neither you nor me have anything to do with their breakup.

We didn't exist in that part of their journey."

Her tone softened, but her clarity became sharper:

"Arjun treated me well.

He respected me.

He was always kind.

I will always support him.

If he ever needs me — ANYTIME — I'll be the first person to help him.

And I will be the first person to clap for his success."

Her loyalty toward him was so transparent, so pure, that even the group stayed quiet.

Then she shifted the phone slightly and said something that melted my heart:

"But Soumya?

I met her later in life.

And she is not walking around with a label.

She is not 'Arjun's ex-girlfriend.'

That is NOT her identity.

She was Soumya before him.

She is Soumya now.

She will always be Soumya."

My eyes instinctively filled with tears.

She didn't stop.

"You ask why I'm still talking to her?"

"Why shouldn't I? What did SHE do wrong?"

Silence.

"She didn't betray anyone.

She didn't hurt anyone.

She didn't insult anyone.

She didn't choose what happened."

She looked directly at the screen and said:

"And tell me this — why should I punish her for someone else's decision?"

It felt like the room paused.

It felt like the world paused.

Then she said something no one expected:

"If she was good enough for Arjun once…

Why is she suddenly not good enough to be treated kindly?"

No one had an answer.

Her voice softened.

"And who knows?

She may become a great friend of mine.

She may bring positivity into my life.

Maybe she will help me grow."

She shrugged lightly.

Two souls can meet ANYTIME in life.

We don't need old labels to block new beginnings."

Then came her final line — the one that silenced everyone:

"She is harmless.

To me.

To Arjun.

To all of you.

So what exactly are you protecting us from?"

There was pin-drop silence.

The movie kept playing in the background, but we weren't watching anymore.

Manasa had spoken with such grace, maturity, and fierce honesty that I felt something inside me shift.

It felt like a divine moment — not dramatic, but powerful.

I looked at her, and a thought struck me:

Is this how Krishna defended Arjuna?

Is this how divine protection feels?

Not loud.

Not violent.

Just truth spoken with love.

In that moment, she had two choices:

She could have played it safe.

She could have said, "Yes, maybe I should avoid Soumya."

She could have protected her image.

She could have chosen the majority.

She could have chosen silence — the easiest escape.

But she didn't.

She didn't choose comfort.

She chose a character.

She didn't choose fear.

She chose the truth.

She didn't choose what people expected.

She chose what her heart told her was right.

And that day, I understood:

Kindness is never disloyalty.

Choosing someone in pain is not betraying someone else.

Real loyalty is not about sides — it's about integrity.

Slowly… very slowly…

Something beautiful happened.

Those same friends who questioned her,

who hesitated around me,

who maintained distance…

began seeing the real me.

They smiled more openly.

They spoke more warmly.

They cracked jokes.

They included me in conversations.

They apologised in their own silent ways.

They did NOT become my best friends.

And they didn't have to.

But they stopped judging.

Stopped assuming.

Stopped creating boundaries.

They just saw me as I really am — Soumya.

Not a title.

Not a tag.

Not a past story.

And I didn't judge them either.

Everyone acts from their level of awareness.

At that time, they didn't know me.

They knew "a story," not the person.

Through Manasa, the universe gave all of us a new perspective.

Maybe I came into that group not for acceptance,

but as a lesson.

Maybe it was meant to teach them not to judge too quickly.

Maybe Manasa was sent into my life to teach me loyalty,

but maybe I was sent into hers to teach her courage.

Maybe this entire situation was a divine test:

Fear of abandonment

vs

Strength of truth

No one tried to blame her.

No one tried to scare her into changing.

People didn't corner her or question her endlessly.

They just… let her be.

They understood her in their own quiet way.

They respected what she chose.

And they stayed.

That's when it hit me —

strength doesn't always look bold.

Sometimes it's barely visible.

Sometimes it just sits there, steady, and slowly changes everything around it.

Manasa was like that.

She didn't shout to be heard.

She didn't argue just to win.

She didn't give explanations to prove her worth.

She simply said what she felt, the way she felt it.

And somehow, people listened — not because they had to,

but because they wanted to.

Watching her, I understood something I had never fully understood before:

fear makes you cautious, guarded, always calculating your next step.

But love…

love makes you show up, even when your hands are shaking.

Love makes you braver than fear ever allows you to be.

Character makes you divine.

And Manasa?

She was all three —

Brave, loving… and quietly divine.

Her presence didn't just help me cope.

It actually healed me in ways I didn't even realise at the time.

Because healing doesn't always come through big moments or dramatic acts.

Sometimes it comes from one simple thing —

someone choosing you when they really don't have to.

Manasa chose me.

And somehow, that quiet choice changed the direction of my life.

Even now, I truly believe this —

the world didn't change for me first.

I changed.

Slowly.

In small ways.

Almost without noticing.

And only after that did the world begin to respond differently to me.

This shift wasn't sudden.

It didn't feel magical when it was happening.

It came through the tiniest wins —

the habits I stuck to,

the promises I kept to myself,

the effort I showed up with even on days I didn't feel like it.

Just small things, done again and again.

Those small things quietly started adding up.

And one day, without any announcement or celebration,

they became the biggest change of my life.

That's when I finally understood something simple but powerful:

you don't need to fix your whole life at once.

You just need to change one small thing inside you, every day.

The rest…

life somehow finds its own way to meet you halfway.

Chapter 10

THE FIRST TIME I TRUSTED CALM

There was one evening I remember very clearly — the first time I truly felt how much he had started to matter to me.

It was a small thing.

So small that, on any other day, I wouldn't have even noticed it.

I had sent him a voice note after a long, exhausting day.

Nothing dramatic.

Just me talking about how tired I felt and how everything inside me felt heavy for no clear reason.

He saw it.

But he didn't reply.

Minutes passed.

Then an hour.

Then two.

My mind began to travel faster than my heart could keep up.

"Maybe he's busy."

Then —

"Maybe I said something wrong."

Then —

"Maybe I'm expecting too much."

Then —

"Maybe I don't matter as much as I think I do."

Old fears know exactly how to disguise themselves as logic.

By the time he finally replied, I was already closed off.

He said gently:

"Sorry, I got caught in something. Are you okay now?"

But my tone had changed.

I replied with fewer words.

Short sentences.

No emotion.

He sensed it immediately.

"Did I upset you?"

I wanted to say no.

I wanted to be calm.

But instead, the truth slipped out softly:

"I felt ignored."

There was silence after that.

Not the uncomfortable kind.

The thoughtful kind.

Then he said something I did not expect.

"I didn't know that would affect you this much. I should've told you I'd be late. I'm sorry."

That moment confused me.

Because in the past, my feelings were often defended against.

Explained away.

Minimised.

But here… they were simply accepted.

Still, I felt vulnerable.

So I said, very quietly:

"I don't like feeling like this. It scares me."

He replied:

"I don't want to be someone who scares you. I want to be someone you feel safe with."

We didn't talk much after that.

We both took some space.

That night, I lay on my bed thinking:

"Why did this affect me so deeply?"

"We are not even together."

"So why does his silence shake me so much?"

And that's when I understood something honestly for the first time:

I cared.

Not in a dramatic way.

Not in an attached, desperate way.

But in a real, human way.

The next morning, he texted first.

"Good morning. I hope today feels lighter."

That was it.

No long explanation.

No justifications.

No ego.

Just softness.

And something inside me relaxed.

We didn't need to rehash the fight.

We didn't need to prove who was right.

We just returned to each other — gently.

Later that day, I asked him:

"Why didn't you get angry yesterday?"

He said:

"Because you weren't attacking me. You were just hurting. There's a difference."

That line stayed with me.

From that day on, I stopped fearing disagreement with him.

Because I realised we weren't fighting to protect our egos.

We were speaking to protect the bond.

Our conflicts were not about who would win.

They were about how we would stay.

And that changed everything.

Beautiful. Here is the **second conflict**, showing your inner shift, exactly in the tone of your journey — calmer, aware, evolved:

It was a day when I really needed him.

Not dramatically.

Just emotionally.

I had returned from a long day where everything felt off.

Nothing had gone wrong, but nothing felt right either.

One of those strange days where your heart feels heavy for no visible reason.

I texted him:

"Are you free today?"

He replied a few minutes later:

"I have some work and then plans with my friends. I'll call you later, okay?"

That's all he said.

Simple.

Honest.

There was a time when that line alone would've shaken me.

My chest would tighten.

My thoughts would spiral.

"Why are his friends more important today?"

"Why am I not the priority?"

"Why do I feel pushed aside?"

Earlier, this would've turned into panic.

Into insecurity.

Into assumption.

But this time… something different happened.

I felt the emotion rise.

I noticed it.

And I paused.

For the first time in my life, I didn't react immediately.

Inside my head, two voices spoke.

The old one said:

"See? You always come second."

The new one said:

"Breathe. This is not abandonment. This is just life."

And for the first time —

I chose the new one.

I simply replied:

"Okay. Have a good time. Talk later."

And that was it.

No games.

No silent waiting.

No checking my phone every few minutes with a knot in my chest.

I stepped out for a walk.

Came back and made myself dinner.

Watched something easy, something that didn't demand emotion.

Wrote a little in my journal.

Let the evening move at its own pace.

Later that night, he called.

Before I could even say much, he said,

"Thank you for understanding today. It really meant a lot."

I smiled when I heard that.

Because this time, I actually did understand.

Not out of fear.

And that was it.

No testing.

No hidden expectations.

No waiting by the phone with anxiety.

I went for a walk.

Made myself dinner.

Watched a TV show.

Sat with my journal.

Let the evening pass peacefully.

I told him honestly:

"There was a time when this would've upset me. But I'm learning not to panic anymore."

He went quiet for a second.

Then said softly:

"I can feel that change in you."

That one sentence felt like a reward for all the inner work I had been doing silently.

But the real conflict came a few days later.

We misunderstood each other over something small.

A tone.

A delay.

A feeling that didn't get expressed properly.

He thought I was pulling away.

I thought he was being distant.

Earlier, this kind of situation would've turned into:

Long messages.

Clarifications.

Defensiveness.

Over-explaining.

Tears.

But this time, I remembered what I had been practicing:

"If I already know the ending… how would I act today?"

So instead of reacting,

I called him.

Not to cry.

Not to accuse.

Just to talk.

I said calmly:

"I think we've misunderstood each other. Can we clear it?"

There was a pause on the other side.

Then he said:

"I was hoping you'd do this instead of getting upset."

We spoke.

Slowly.

Honestly.

Without ego.

And in the middle of that conversation, I realised something that surprised even me:

I was not afraid of losing him.

I wanted him.

I valued him.

But I was no longer terrified of disappearance.

Because somewhere, I had finally learned:

I would still be okay.

And that changed the energy between us completely.

After that call, he said something that still echoes in me:

"You're different now. You don't fight to be held. You stand steadily. And that makes me want to hold you more."

That night, I didn't overthink.

I didn't analyse.

I didn't replay.

I slept.

This time, the conflict did not stem from fear.

It came from growth.

And that is how our bond slowly shifted —

Not with fireworks.

Not with dramatic confessions.

But with emotional maturity.

Little by little.

Day by day.

We were still not in a relationship.

But we were no longer "just friends" either.

Something deeper was forming —

Not out of attachment,

But out of choice.

One of the things I always admired about Karthik — even before anything started— was his honesty in the smallest things.

We were just normal friends back then.

No expectations.

No emotional weight.

No silent hopes.

It was his birthday.

I remember calling him in the evening.

We spoke for a long time — about random things, about how his day went, about nothing very serious.

It was one of those easy conversations that feels light and familiar.

Then he said,

"Okay, I'm getting another call. I'll call you later."

I have heard that sentence a hundred times in life.

From people who never really intended to call back.

A polite way to end the conversation.

A soft escape.

For a second, I assumed the same.

I smiled and said,

"Yeah, okay, bye."

And I forgot about it.

But after some time… my phone rang.

It was him.

He called back.

Exactly like he said he would.

I remember smiling without even realising it.

Not because it was something extraordinary.

But because it was honest.

That was his nature.

If he said he would do something, he usually did.

No drama.

No excuses.

No performance.

I liked him as a person because of things like this.

But life doesn't stay in the same phase.

Friendship evolves.

Feelings grow.

Energy shifts.

And with that, expectations silently enter.

As our bond began deepening,

There were days when he would again say,

"I will call you later."

"I'll text you sometime."

And this time, sometimes…

Life would happen.

Work pressure.

Family issues.

Mental exhaustion.

Distractions.

He would forget.

Earlier, even a small thing like that would have shattered me.

My old self would immediately think:

"Did I matter less today?"

"Did he forget me?"

"Am I being taken for granted?"

"Why do I always wait?"

My chest would tighten.

My mind would spiral.

I would sit with my phone in my hand, checking again and again.

But this time…

I noticed something very different in me.

I still felt the emotion.

But I didn't drown in it.

Instead of reacting,

instead of confronting immediately,

instead of assuming,

I paused.

I told myself:

"He is allowed to be human."

"He is allowed to have a life."

"He is allowed to forget sometimes."

"This does not reduce your value."

So I didn't panic.

I didn't send ten messages.

I didn't test him with silence.

I didn't punish him emotionally.

When he called later and said,

"I'm sorry, I completely forgot. It was a crazy day."

I simply said,

"It's okay. I understood."

And I truly meant it.

No bitterness.

No hidden resentment.

No scoreboard in my head.

That is when I understood something powerful about relationships:

Love does not start with romance.

It starts with emotional maturity.

Earlier, I used to measure love by urgency.

Now, I measure it by security.

There were even moments when I told him calmly:

"Next time, don't say you'll call if you're not sure you can. Just say you'll try. That way I don't create expectations."

He listened.

He adapted.

And I did too.

That is how relationships actually evolve —

Not through big fights or dramatic realisations,

but through small conversations,

daily understanding,

and quiet emotional growth.

What I liked about Karthik was not just that he came back when he promised that one day on his birthday.

It was that even when he slipped later,

he owned it.

And I didn't collapse into fear anymore.

We were both learning.

He was learning responsibility.

I was learning trust.

And somewhere between forgotten calls and patient silences,

Our relationship quietly grew stronger.

Not because we were perfect.

But because we were willing to grow.

Healing is slow.

But realisation often arrives in a single, quiet moment.

For me, that moment came with Karthik.

There was always a silent thread between us — something invisible yet unbreakable. A knowing that didn't need reassurance. Some nights, after long walks with Manasa, I would come back to my room, switch off the main light, sit beside the window with only the fairy lights glowing, and wonder why Karthik felt so different from everyone I had known before.

There was no intensity that drained me.

No anxiety that consumed me.

No fear of losing.

There was just… peace.

And peace was something I had searched for my entire life but had never found in a person before.

One evening in Italy, after months of building this new life piece by piece, Karthik and I were on a call. Nothing unusual. Nothing emotional. Just an ordinary conversation. He asked, "How was your day?" and I began telling him everything — about my café shift, how my hands smelled of coffee and vanilla, about my gym session and how I lifted slightly more than yesterday, about the neighbour aunties baking bread again, about how cold the air felt when I walked to class that morning.

And he listened.

Truly listened.

Not waiting for his turn to speak.

Not multitasking.

Not rushing the conversation.

Just being present.

And suddenly, in the middle of that most ordinary conversation, something inside me softened in a way I hadn't expected. A feeling rose quietly within me — not excitement, not attachment… but safety.

"This feels like home."

Not the dramatic, romantic kind of home we see in films.

But the quiet kind.

A home for my nervous system.

A home for my thoughts.

A home for my fears.

A home for my becoming.

He didn't make a grand confession.

He didn't promise anything.

He simply said, calmly and honestly, "I'm proud of you."

And that was enough to shift something within me forever.

That night, I understood a truth I had never understood before:

Love is not what shakes you.

Love is what steadies you.

From there, our bond began to change in subtle ways.

Slowly, our conversations grew warmer.

Deeper.

More intentional.

We were not in a relationship.

But we were no longer just friends either.

It was that beautiful in-between space where two people start seeing each other differently — with softness instead of fear.

There was one day that truly marked my emotional growth.

Karthik had casually said in the morning, "I'll call you in the evening."

Earlier, even that one sentence would have turned into a ticking clock in my chest. By evening, my entire mood would revolve around whether my phone rang or not.

But that day, something was different.

Evening came.

No call.

And yet… I didn't panic.

I cooked myself dinner.

Took a warm shower.

Wrote in my journal.

Let life flow.

It was around 11 at night when my phone finally rang.

It was him.

The first thing he said was, "I'm really sorry. The day got hectic, and I completely lost track of time."

Earlier, my heart would have already created stories. That night, I replied gently, "It's okay. I assumed you must've been busy."

There was a pause.

Then he said softly, "You've changed."

I asked, "In what way?"

And he replied, "You sound… steady."

That word entered me like a blessing.

Steady.

Not anxious.

Not restless.

Not afraid.

Steady.

I smiled and told him, "I think I finally learnt that peace doesn't come from control. It comes from trust."

He didn't respond immediately. Then he said something that stayed with me forever:

"I like this version of you."

That night I realised something profound:

People don't fall in love with your chaos.

They fall in love with your healing.

From that point onward, something matured between us.

We still had emotional moments.

We still had misunderstandings.

We still had silence sometimes.

But they no longer became storms.

We had grown enough to pause.

To reflect.

To respond instead of react.

And that is how our bond evolved — not through labels, not through dramatic declarations, but through emotional growth.

Quiet.

Organic.

Real.

I would overthink.

Assume.

Somewhere between forgotten calls and quiet patience,

Understanding grew.

I realised something important then —

You cannot expect a person to remain exactly the same forever.

Responsibilities change.

Timings change.

Energy changes.

But intention…

That is what matters.

And his intention, even when he faltered, was always clean.

That's how love slowly entered this space —

not loudly, not with fireworks,

but like a soft river that keeps flowing,

changing the land around it without force.

From strangers,

to friends,

to something unnamed yet real.

There was no pressure.

No urgency.

We were simply becoming.

Together.

Chapter 11

THE LOVE THAT TAUGHT ME WHAT'S POSSIBLE

Having someone who feels *your own* — even without labels — does something to you.

It feels warm.

It feels steady.

It feels rare.

This wasn't the first time I had felt closeness,

But this felt different.

More layered.

More complex.

And strangely, because of those complications, I wasn't scared anymore.

Pain has a way of teaching you things no book ever can.

And after everything I had been through, I had realised one truth very clearly —

I didn't just want love.

I wanted *that kind* of love.

There are a couple I know in India — my friend's parents.

They have always been my favourite love story.

When they got married, they had almost nothing.

No comfort.

No financial safety.

Just faith in each other.

During the most challenging phase of his life, when he needed even the smallest support,

My friend's mother would give everything she had —

a pair of earrings, her last bit of savings, anything —

just to keep her husband going.

I often wonder what must have gone on in her heart.

She must have been scared, too.

She must have thought,

What if this also goes? At least I could've kept this for myself.

But she chose something else instead.

She chose to invest in her husband's courage.

In the confidence on his face.

In his becoming.

And maybe she told herself —

What more do I even want from life than this trust, this partnership, this belief in each other?

When the whole world stood away, she stood right beside him.

And you can only imagine the kind of love that grows when two people survive life like that together.

Years passed.

They grew older.

Life changed a thousand times.

But one thing never changed — their respect for each other.

My friend once told me that even in their old age,

her father would still say "I love you" and "thank you" to his wife.

I think that's what kept them together.

Not luck.

Not comfort.

Not perfect circumstances.

They succeed in life not because fortune favoured them.

They succeeded because they favoured each other.

And then one day, he passed away.

I never spoke to him personally,

but when I heard the news, I broke down.

Because I had admired their love from a distance for years.

She was shattered.

She had children to raise.

No great support from the family.

And in this world, people don't always come to help —

Many come to take advantage.

But she stood strong.

So strong.

She raised her children with dignity.

With quiet courage.

With a strength that didn't need to announce itself.

Of course, she misses him every day.

But who said he is gone?

He is only not there physically.

Their love is still alive —

alive enough to give her strength even now.

That is the kind of love I decided I wanted —

or nothing at all.

A love where cheating doesn't even exist as an idea.

A love that stands even when everything else falls apart.

A love that may last a lifetime… or even just a day —

But it is sacred while it lasts.

In our traditions, some people call women who lose their husbands "inauspicious."

I hate that belief with every part of me.

If anything, I would take blessings from a woman who has experienced a love like that

over those who never knew what real love meant.

Purity isn't about rituals.

It's about how deeply you can love,

how gently you can bless another life.

That is the kind of blessing I want.

And that day, with all of this in my heart,

I quietly asked the universe for nothing dramatic —

just this:

If love is to come into my life again, let it be real.

Let it be brave.

Let it be the kind that stands.

And that was when the universe responded.

THE CALL THAT SAID EVERYTHING WITHOUT SAYING MUCH

Karthik messaged me first.

Not casually.

Not like he usually did.

There was something different —

something urgent and raw in his tone.

He asked if we could talk.

When we got on the call, he didn't rush into anything.

He spoke slowly, carefully — as if searching for the right words.

Then he said it.

Something so simple…

yet so heavy that it stopped my heartbeat for a moment:

"Come back soon…

I want to see who you're becoming."

For a second, I didn't even react.

Not because I didn't hear him —

But because I felt the intention behind those words.

He didn't say:

"Come back for me."

"Come back so we can be together."

"Come back so we can start something new."

He said:

"Come back so I can witness your becoming."

That sentence alone showed the entire truth of his heart.

A man who is not afraid of your growth.

A man who doesn't feel insecure about your progress.

A man who wants to walk beside you,

not in front of you,

not behind you.

And that's when I knew:

Karthik wasn't someone I would outgrow.

He was someone I would grow with.

THE KNOWING THAT THIS SHOULD STAY

After that call, something settled inside me —

something that had never settled with anyone else.

A quiet knowing.

He never asked,

never pressured,

never demanded.

But still, I felt seen.

Understood.

Chosen in the most graceful way possible.

I kept replaying his words in my mind:

"I want to see who you're becoming."

That one line carried acceptance,

trust,

respect,

and grounding.

It wasn't a confession.

It was a promise —

unspoken, but unmistakable.

THE DECISION TO COME HOME

My 1.5 years in Italy were ending,

and for the first time since landing there,

I didn't feel like I was leaving something behind.

I felt like I was going *towards* something.

Europe gave me growth.

Manasa gave me strength.

But India had something else waiting for me.

My family,

my roots,

my career path,

my next chapter…

and yes —

Karthik.

Not because I wanted to depend on him.

Not because I was scared of distance.

Not because I wanted a relationship to fill an empty space.

But because something divine pulled me back.

A whisper inside me said:

"You and Karthik have a chapter to write.

This isn't over."

I asked myself honestly:

"I know I can fight for someone I love…

But will he fight for me?"

I didn't want to ask him.

I didn't want to test him.

I didn't want to force anything.

If love is real,

it reveals itself naturally.

It fights naturally.

It stays naturally.

So, I prayed again:

"God...

If Karthik truly loves me,

Please give him strength.

Remove his fear.

Fill him with clarity and courage.

I will fight a thousand battles for the man I love and his family...

I want him to fight one battle for me."

After that night,

I stopped worrying.

I stopped overthinking.

I surrendered the whole story to God.

And that's when everything aligned effortlessly.

The night before I flew to India,

We spoke again.

Just casual things —

luggage, airports, weather, food.

But then he said:

"When you come… everything will make sense."

And with that one sentence,

every anxiety I had about the future disappeared.

There was no confusion.

No resistance.

Just a deep, quiet knowing:

This should stay.

This deserves a chance.

This is written by something bigger than us.

THE FINAL DAYS IN ITALY — PACKING A VERSION OF MYSELF

When I told my parents over a late-night video call,

"Amma… Daddy… I'm coming back to India."

Their faces lit up instantly.

My mother's smile was so wide she forgot to blink.

My father's eyes softened, as they do only when he is truly happy.

Even over a glitchy network and pixelated screen, I could feel their excitement.

They began planning instantly —

what I should eat the day I land,

who would pick me up,

how they would redecorate my room,

which relatives to inform,

and how early they should leave for the airport.

For a moment, I felt like a ten-year-old girl going home from a school trip —

not a woman returning after 1.5 years of breaking and rebuilding herself.

Telling them made everything real.

I was going home.

Not as the Soumya who left —

but as someone they had never met before.

THE PACKING — STUFFING MEMORIES AND PARTS OF MYSELF INTO SUITCASES

Packing looks simple from the outside —

zipper, clothes, chargers, shoes.

But for Manasa and me, packing felt like packing an entire era.

My room turned into a storm —
open suitcases on the bed,

clothes scattered on the floor,
books stacked in uneven piles,

half-used candles,

old metro tickets,

scribbled notes,

aprons from baking class,

coffee shop caps,

tiny fridge magnets,

and dried flowers pressed inside my journals.

Manasa came over with her bun half-tied,

holding chips in one hand and tape in the other.

"Let's finish this tonight," she announced,

as if we were going into battle.

We folded clothes together,

argued about what I should throw,

laughed at how many outfits we bought impulsively,

and paused multiple times,

just looking at each other with that heavy feeling of

"This is ending."

She helped me wrap fragile things in bubble wrap,

label boxes,

clean drawers,

and tuck away memories.

Every time I closed a suitcase,

It felt like closing a chapter.

We walked to a nearby friend's apartment to say goodbye.

A small group gathered —

friends from class, café, and part-time shifts.

We took pictures,

hugged tightly,

promised to stay in touch,

and for a moment, the entire year flashed before my eyes.

Manasa was supposed to come a month later.

She kept saying,

"Go ahead… I'll join you soon. Don't cry now."

But something about leaving her felt heavier than I expected.

We didn't say goodbye —

We just said,

"See you in a month,"

the way people say "see you tomorrow,"

because we couldn't accept the truth of the distance.

THE FLIGHT — THOUGHTS THAT WOULDN'T LET ME SLEEP

On the plane, I stared out the window

at the blurry night lights of Italy shrinking into shadows.

My mind was louder than the engine.

I thought about Arjun.

I thought about how much I tried,

how I fought silently,

How I stayed loyal,

How I protected the relationship more than myself.

There were so many chances to walk away

So many reasons to give up

so many battles we *could* have fought for each other…

But we didn't.

Maybe because we weren't meant to.

Maybe because he didn't see what I saw.

Maybe because we weren't designed to be each other's "forever."

Then I thought of Karthik.

The difference shocked me.

With Arjun, even small hurdles felt big.

With Karthik, even big hurdles felt small.

With Arjun, everything needed effort.

With Karthik, everything felt natural.

Even with a hundred reasons to run away,

He stayed.

Even with a hundred obstacles between us —
caste, religion, parents, expectations —

I felt, deep in my heart,
that he was willing to fight for me.

He never said,

"I will fight for you."

He never made grand declarations.

But his actions whispered it.

His consistency screamed it.

His presence proved it.

And that's when I remembered something my from a book I read:

"A man changes for a woman only when he sees divinity in her presence."

I smiled to myself in that dim, cold aeroplane seat.

Because that was exactly what was happening.

WHAT MAKES A MAN FIGHT FOR A WOMAN — THE TRUTH I LEARNED

This part deserves its own spotlight.

Because every woman deserves to know it.

Men don't fight for you because you're beautiful.

Not because you're perfect.

Not because you cook well or look good or behave "correctly."

A man fights for you when:

1. He sees peace in your presence.

Not drama.

Not chaos.

Not confusion.

You become his safe space —

the one place in the world where he feels understood.

2. He sees the woman you are becoming, not just the woman you are now.

A real man looks at you

and sees your potential,

your fire,

your softness,

your future.

3. He respects your character.

Respect grows love more than romance ever will.

With you, Karthik saw honesty,

depth,

loyalty,

and emotional strength.

4. He feels that life with you will expand him.

Men fight for women who make them better human beings.

With Arjun, everything was survival.

With Karthik, everything was growing.

5. He knows losing you would be his biggest regret.

Not because he's scared of being alone,

but because he knows your energy is one-of-a-kind.

And the most important:

6. His soul recognises yours.

Destiny isn't loud.

It doesn't scream.

It whispers.

And when a man listens to that whisper,

he becomes brave

in ways he never expected.

Even if he is from an orthodox family.

Even if he was raised with strict rules.

Even if he has fears.

Even if the world tells him, "it's impossible."

A man will fight for the woman who awakens something sacred in him.

And as I sat in that aeroplane,

hands cold,

heart warm,

I realised:

Karthik wasn't fighting me.

He was fighting his fears — for me.

And that's what makes a man worth loving.

Chapter 12

COMING HOME TO A NEW VERSION OF MYSELF

After spending 1.5 years in Italy, when I boarded the flight back home, a strange mix of excitement and softness rested quietly inside me. I wasn't the same woman who had left India. Italy didn't just give me memories—it restructured me internally, layer by layer, belief by belief.

I had worked on the six major areas of my life—health, relationships, career, family, friendships, and money.

Was I perfect?

No.

But I wasn't the version who left crying either.

I had moved from survival to awareness.

From fear to intention.

From confusion to clarity.

I had become someone who *believed* she could grow.

That belief alone felt like the biggest achievement.

When the plane touched down in Bangalore, it felt like a soft bell ringing somewhere inside my heart, saying:

"You're home… but not the same."

I was excited to meet everyone—my family, my friends… and yes, Karthik.

A part of me was nervous too, but not in a negative way—more like meeting someone special after becoming someone new.

I walked past the sliding doors of the airport, dragging my suitcase with sleepy eyes and a tired smile. And then, suddenly, everything inside me paused.

There he was.

Karthik.

Standing with flowers.

Waiting like it was the most natural thing in the world.

His eyes carried a warmth I hadn't seen in anyone in a very long time—almost like he had been waiting not just for me to land, but for my heart to land too.

In that moment, something very important settled inside me:

When a bond is real, you don't need to hold on to it.

It holds on to you.

Distance didn't dilute anything between us—

It distilled it.

Purified it.

Strengthened it.

People always say toxic relationships are difficult.

But that's not true.

Healthy relationships are more challenging

—because they won't let you run.

They won't let you hide behind wounds.

They won't allow silence to replace communication.

They hold up a mirror and ask you to grow.

And honestly,

real love is far more terrifying than chaos,

because real love asks you to become better.

Karthik's presence felt something like God Himself placed gently into my life.

I didn't plan to come back to India *for* him,

but somewhere inside, I knew his presence was part of the reason I was returning.

Some chapters can only be written in the same country—

with physical presence, shared days, shared breaths, shared life.

By then, both of us already knew how compatible we were.

Not in forced ways, not in dramatic ways—

just naturally, effortlessly, divinely.

There were no grand promises in the beginning.

Nothing rushed.

Nothing projected into the future.

And ironically, that's exactly how I knew this was written by something bigger than the both of us.

He waited.

I waited.

We let the connection grow the way a flower opens—

slowly, tenderly, at its own pace.

And in that space…

For the first time in my life, love didn't scare me.

Love made me feel safe.

We both had pasts—

But we didn't hold each other prisoner to them.

We saw each other as two souls meeting at the right time after learning the right lessons.

He became the stillness in my chaos.

The voice that said, "You can."

The person whose presence calmed everything inside me.

He once told me, "I never thought I'd fight for a girl."

And that made me smile because

a man only fights when he sees divinity, not desperation.

Growing up with divine love stories—Shiva-Shakti, Rama-Sita, Radha-Krishna—I always dreamt of marrying someone in whom I saw God. Not literally, but energetically—

purity, loyalty, strength, warmth, and courage.

With Karthik, I felt all of this naturally… almost effortlessly.

Those 1.5 years apart didn't damage anything.

If anything, they helped us realise each other's value

in a deeper, more soul-level way.

If someone asked me who Karthik was to me, I'd say:

He is the one man whose core personality made every other man I knew look ordinary.

And still, in all this clarity,

there was a practical reality waiting—marriage.

My parents hinted at it multiple times while I was in Europe.

Not because of age or pressure,

but because they wanted me to be secure and happy.

But I've always been clear about one thing:

I will NEVER marry because "it is time."

I will marry when it feels true.

When I know the person, not his background.

With Karthik, the conversation of marriage came up naturally.

Calmly.

Lovingly.

With depth.

But his parents were orthodox and strict.

He never took a step earlier because he didn't want to hurt them.

But distance changes people.

Pain brings clarity.

Silence brings truth.

Time brings maturity.

And somewhere in all of this,

We realised that mutual love between two people from different worlds

It's never an accident.

God doesn't create mutual energy without a possibility.

So without rushing anything,

without forcing anything,

we simply trusted what destiny was doing.

When I decided to return to India…

I felt something inside me whisper:

"You and Karthik have a chapter to write.

This story isn't done."

The Actual Moment — When the Plane Landed

Once he saw me,

I didn't overthink.

I didn't act shy.

I just walked up to him and hugged him.

Effortlessly.

Like my body recognised him before my mind did.

We spoke for almost an hour at the airport—

about the flight, food, my luggage struggles, plans,

and random things that didn't matter but felt warm.

After that, he had to leave for some work,

and I had to catch a bus to my hometown.

We planned to meet again in a day or two.

No drama.

No big proposal.

No over-the-top promises.

Just two aligned souls meeting again after 18 months—

comfortably, naturally, peacefully.

I don't want to compare or degrade anyone from my past.

Arjun was a chapter.

Karthik is another.

Both served different roles in my life's journey.

But I can say this with honesty:

This moment with Karthik felt like coming home to myself.

The New Soumya Who Returned

Earlier, whenever something beautiful happened in my life,

I used to get scared.

"What if I lose all this?"

"What if something goes wrong?"

"What if happiness doesn't stay?"

But something had shifted inside me.

This time, I wasn't scared.

I felt nervous, yes—because I cared.

But not scared.

Italy changed something in my identity.

I stopped believing that happiness is fragile.

I started believing that

even if I lose everything, I can pick it all up again.

Because now I knew who I was capable of becoming.

And that realisation came from something deeper:

deservability.

Growing up, I was constantly told—

"Don't get too excited, you might lose it."

"Don't ask for too much, it won't come true."

"Keep quiet, don't dream too big."

Those beliefs buried my self-worth.

Made me think happiness was unstable.

Made me feel undeserving of good things.

But healing showed me the opposite.

You lose things when you chase from fear.

You lose things when you put them on a pedestal.

You lose things when you make outcomes bigger than yourself.

And for the first time,

I didn't feel that fear.

I didn't feel like clinging.

I didn't feel like controlling.

I felt… aligned.

With that feeling,

I got into my cab and left for home—

carrying my suitcase,

my journal,

and a brand new version of myself.

Coming Home — And Seeing Everything With New Eyes

When I reached home, I didn't realise how emotional it would feel — not just for me, but for everyone who watched me walk through that door after one and a half years.

My mom saw me first.

She didn't cry dramatically, nothing filmy…

She just stood there for two seconds, trying to process that I was actually home.

Then she smiled — that kind of smile mothers give only twice in life:

When we're born, and when we come back after life has changed us.

She hugged me tightly, her hands lingering on my back as if checking whether I'd eaten well, slept well, survived well.

My dad came out of the room pretending to be casual —

"How are youuu? How was your flight?"

But the way he kept staring at my face said everything he wouldn't put into words.

My Brother ran from the hallway, shouting my name like I was some celebrity returning from a world tour.

He grabbed my suitcase, opened it without permission, and immediately went hunting for chocolates.

That's how he expresses love.

Even our dog — the only creature who loves with zero confusion —

came running, barking, jumping, sniffing, almost scolding me for going missing for so long.

I didn't realise how much I missed that sound until that moment.

I spent the first two days at home feeling like I'd stepped into a warm, familiar dream.

Nothing had changed.

The same faded sofa with slightly crooked cushions.

The same curtains flutter with the same breeze.

The same kitchen sounds — mom's vessels, the cooker whistle, and dad asking where his glasses are.

The same evening, the chai smell.

The same neighbourhood voices floating through the window.

The same life.

But I had changed.

When I walked out of this house one and a half years ago,

I carried a heart that was shattered in quiet ways —

a heart that didn't know where to go or how to feel or who it was becoming.

Now, when I walked back in,

I carried a heart that was slowly pieced together —

not perfect, but grounded, steadier, softer, stronger.

Everyone looked at me and said the usual things:

"You look exactly the same!"

Tell us everything about your Europe

"Masters got over, but you're still our old Soumya."

And I smiled — not because they were right,

but because they didn't know the quiet truth.

Yes, maybe my face looked the same.

Maybe my hair hadn't changed.

Maybe I came back with the same voice, same laugh, same mannerisms.

Maybe all I visibly gained was a degree.

But what they couldn't see was this:

The real shift was inside me.

And that changed everything.

When we are low, we think our entire world needs to change —

new place, new people, new life.

But the truth is:

The version of us who is confident, powerful, calm, and capable…

already exists within us.

We just haven't met her yet.

And this homecoming taught me something:

Healing doesn't make you unrecognisable.

It just makes you **more you** than ever before.

The Internal Shift That Changes Your Entire Reality

When you are at your lowest, there is something important you must understand — something I learned the hard way:

The strongest, most confident, most powerful version of you already exists.

Not in the future.

Not somewhere far away.

Not after ten years.

Right now.

You just haven't tapped into her yet.

Just like how I wrote my story —

You can write yours too.

In my past relationship, my entire happiness depended on one person.

My emotional stability, my peace, my joy — everything sat on one pair of shoulders.

Now… it doesn't.

Now, if someone enters my life, they add to my happiness — but they are not the source of it.

I finally know how to take care of myself.

I finally know how to slow down and enjoy the moment.

The moment I made that internal shift, *my entire external world began to look different.*

Have you ever watched a movie where:

No matter how many twists come…

No matter how complicated things get…

You *somehow know* the hero and heroine are going to end up together?

Or the family will eventually agree?

Or the conflict will resolve?

You don't panic.

You don't doubt.

You don't overthink.

Why?

Because you already know the ending.

That's the kind of conviction we need to have in the story *we* write about our own life.

But here is where we go wrong:

When we think about something that has already happened, we feel no anxiety — because we know the outcome.

But when we think about the future, even if it's something we deeply desire, we don't hold that same conviction.

We think:

What if it doesn't work?

What if something goes wrong?

What if the universe doesn't support me?

And here's the truth:

Your mind doesn't know the past or the future.

It only knows NOW.

It only reads the emotion you are holding right this moment.

So if you think about your future with doubt, fear, or hesitation,

then that becomes your vibration.

But if you think about your future the way you think about your past — with FULL certainty —

Then everything starts to shift.

Let me give you an example.

Think about a childhood memory —

maybe your first day of school,

or a family vacation,

Or the day you learned to ride a bicycle.

When you think about it now,

There is **zero fear**,

zero doubt,

zero discomfort.

Why?

Because you *know* it happened.

Your mind has no confusion about it.

It holds that memory with pure conviction.

Now imagine thinking about your future in the exact same way.

The house you want.

The job you want.

The peace you want.

The relationship you want.

The love you want with Karthik.

Imagine thinking about them as if they have **already happened**.

The mind does not know the difference between

memory and *imagination*.

It only responds to conviction.

When you think of your future with the same certainty you feel about your past,

your mind shifts,

your energy shifts,

your behaviour shifts,

and eventually…

Your reality shifts.

That is when the universe aligns things you once thought were impossible

When it comes to Karthik, I want to believe the same way:

That everything is going to work out.

That every hurdle will be crossed.

That love will win.

That the universe is not small or weak.

That divine timing is real.

I don't want to underestimate the universe's ability.

I want to believe that what is written for us will happen — naturally, peacefully, beautifully.

And for the first time in my life,

I am not scared of losing something good.

Because now I know:

Even if I lose everything,

I know how to pick myself up again.

I know how to rebuild.

I know how to heal.

I know how to trust myself.

And that is the difference.

That is why I no longer panic when something goes wrong.

I no longer fear the "what if."

Because now I know:

I am not fragile anymore.

I am someone who was broke once…

but rebuilt herself in a foreign country —

and returned home stronger, calmer, wiser, and far more aligned with her truth.

The version of me that stands here today

is someone I once prayed to become.

And if I can write this story for myself,

So can you.

Chapter 13

WHEN FAITH BECAME OUR FIGHT

After I came back to India, something between Karthik and me changed — not suddenly, not dramatically, but surely. It wasn't exciting. It wasn't a rush. It was a calm certainty settling into both our hearts at the same time.

We didn't wake up one day and say, *"Let's get married."*

It didn't happen like that.

It happened slowly, in silence, in long pauses after conversations ended, in the way we looked at each other when we spoke about life, in the quiet truth that neither of us could imagine a future where the other wasn't present in some way.

One evening, we were sitting together without saying much. There was no big conversation happening. Just the sound of traffic outside, two cups of untouched coffee between us, and a heaviness in the air that didn't feel scary — it felt sacred.

And then, very simply, I said,

"Whatever happens… I can't see my life with anyone else."

He didn't respond immediately. He just looked at me for a long time — not with excitement, not with fear, but with that rare seriousness that comes when a person knows a decision is no longer optional.

Finally, he said quietly,

“I feel the same. And that’s exactly why this scares me. Because when something matters this much… you don’t treat it casually.”

That’s when we both knew.

This wasn’t about romance anymore.

This was about choice.

This was about responsibility.

This was about believing in a union even when the odds didn’t look kind.

We didn’t say, *“Everything will be easy.”*

We said, *“Even if it’s hard, we will try.”*

Even if there was only **0.1% hope**, we were willing to bet our entire faith on that one fraction. Because sometimes, when love is real, even a tiny possibility feels bigger than a hundred logical reasons to walk away.

There was no fighting in our decision.

There was only belief.

I kept telling my friends something very simple:

When parents oppose a love marriage, most of the time it doesn’t come from hatred.

It comes from **fear**.

Fear that we might be making a wrong choice.

Fear that we might suffer.

Fear of society.

Fear of unfamiliar paths.

Fear of what they cannot control.

They don't really reject the person we love.

They reject the **unknown**.

Because they haven't lived our moments.

They haven't heard our conversations.

They haven't seen how we hold each other during silence.

They haven't witnessed the growth, the pain, the healing, the alignment.

They only see caste.

Religion.

Community.

"What will people say?"

But when *you* don't believe in what your heart has chosen…

When *you* refuse to fight for what feels sacred to you…

Then what is the point of living honestly?

Convincing parents is never about proving them wrong in a day.

It is about slowly showing them — through consistency, character, and stability — that the decision came from wisdom, not madness.

And in that journey, more than arguments, what you need is **each other's back**.

In such a powerful way that even God feels like stepping in and softening everything.

Karthik and I made one silent pact that day:

We will not fight the world with words.

We will fight it with growth.

We both felt that if we reached a stage in life where people were forced to look at us beyond today…

Beyond our current position,

Beyond our current limitations,

Beyond superficial labels…

Then all these walls would look small on their own.

So we decided to **grow first**.

To grow professionally.

To grow in stability.

To grow in strength.

To grow in respect.

Not to impress society —

But to remove every excuse society hides behind.

I faced a lot of pressure because of my age.

A lot of subtle taunts.

A lot of silent judgments.

A lot of *"It's time now, you shouldn't wait."*

But deep inside, I was calm.

Because I knew what I was fighting for.

And I knew the worth of it.

I accepted that pain —

just like a mother accepts the pain of childbirth

to give birth to a beautiful life.

I knew I was giving birth to a future.

And that birth would hurt.

But one thing was crystal clear inside me:

The day I get married,

It should be **Karthik beside me**.

Not because life forced me.

Not because age pushed me.

Not because fear cornered me.

But because my soul chose him — fully, consciously, without doubt.

And Karthik felt the same.

That kind of mutual knowing doesn't come from excitement.

It comes from **alignment**.

From two people standing in their truth and saying,

"Even if the whole world questions us…

We won't question each other."

And that's how our decision was born —

not out of desperation,

not out of rebellion,

but out of **deep, quiet, unshakable belief**.

After everything that was said and everything that was felt, Karthik and I made one clear decision together:

We will grow.

Not just in love.

Not just in emotion.

But in life.

We decided that if our parents were to accept us one day, it should never be out of compulsion. It should never be because they felt cornered. It should never be because "time ran out."

I didn't want his parents to accept me because they had no choice.

I wanted them to accept me because they *wanted to*.

I wanted Karthik to receive the same love I receive from my people.

And I wanted to receive the same love he receives from his.

I wanted his parents to look at me one day and say —

"She is our daughter too."

Without fear.

Without pressure.

Without hesitation.

And I knew one thing —

That kind of love cannot be demanded.

It must be *earned through being.*

I was ready to do anything for that.

Not to prove myself.

But to become the kind of woman who felt unquestionable in her presence.

It wasn't easy.

Some days, it felt exhausting.

But love that is meant to last is never built on convenience.

It is built on character.

And this is something I tell every man and woman who truly loves:

If you really love someone and you want your family to understand your love, try one thing.

Just once.

Go to your mother and speak exactly the way your heart feels.

Not with arguments.

Not with logic.

But with emotion.

Tell her why this person feels safe.

Tell her why this person feels right.

Tell her who you become when you are with them.

Tell her what kind of peace this person brings into your life.

Don't talk about caste.

Don't talk about religion.

Don't talk about society.

Talk about *love.*

Because a mother understands love better than anyone in this world.

Behind every resistance is only one thing —

Fear.

Fear that their child might suffer.

Fear that their child might be hurt.

Fear that their child might be choosing the wrong path.

And fear does not dissolve with logic.

Fear dissolves with truth.

As we grow up, we forget one thing —

Our parents were once young, too.

They loved it too.

They dreamed too.

They feared too.

They are not our enemies.

They are just scared guardians of a world they don't fully understand anymore.

I heard this story once,

and it stayed with me in a way I can't explain.

"A king never begs for a queen.

He builds a kingdom that is worthy of her."

When a man truly wants a woman to be his queen, he doesn't fight only with words.

He fights with growth.

With discipline.

With self-respect.

With elevation.

A king does not give excuses.

He gives a future.

A king never thinks of what he will lose.

He thinks of what he will build.

And when he builds his kingdom — no matter how small, no matter how humble — the queen chooses to live there because she feels safe.

And history is full of such love.

Shiva and Parvati —

Where the world rejected him, she chose him.

Where society judged him, she meditated for him.

Akbar and Jodha —

Two religions, one empire of trust.

Salim and Anarkali —

Love that dared to exist in the middle of a kingdom.

These stories survived centuries not because they were easy —

But because they were *brave.*

When a man wants his queen, he builds a kingdom big enough to protect her from the world.

And when a woman trusts a man, she walks into that kingdom even when it is still under construction.

That is not romance.

That is legacy.

I began to notice small changes in Karthik… quiet ones, but meaningful.
Not because I asked him to.
But because love has that effect on a man.
It sharpens him.
It wakes him up.
It makes him aware of his own potential.
As he started growing in his career, something else began to happen too.
Jealousy.
Some of his friends — the same ones who used to cheer him when he was casual, laid-back, and harmless — suddenly grew distant.
They laughed less.
They supported less.

They envied more.

When he first noticed it, he was confused.

"Why are they behaving like this?" he asked me one night.

And I told him one simple truth:

"What they hate in you is missing in them."

People celebrate your comfort.

But they struggle to celebrate your ambition.

They are happiest when you are at their level.

But they feel threatened the moment you rise.

Not everyone who walks with you in the beginning deserves to walk with you to the top.

He didn't want to believe it at first.

Because he is kind.

And kind people always look for goodness in others.

But slowly, reality began to show itself.

Some people around him didn't know how to handle his growth.
One friend started downplaying his achievements.
Another mocked his discipline.
One tried to distract him whenever he focused on work.
Someone else made him feel guilty for "changing."

But there were others too —
the ones who quietly encouraged him,
who noticed his effort,
who were genuinely happy for his progress,
who pushed him forward instead of pulling him back.
Not everyone drifted.
Some people stood by him with the same loyalty he offered them.

I think phases like these teach you everything you need to know about relationships —
who is real,

who truly wants to see you win,
and who only liked the version of you that stayed small.

One evening he came to me and said softly,
"I think I'm outgrowing people."

I held his hand and replied,
"No… you're growing.
Some people will grow with you,
and some won't.
That's just life."

When things are good, everyone feels like the perfect companion.
But when you evolve,
the people around you either rise with you…
or drift away on their own.

And accepting that truth is a part of every person's journey.

The other struggles came with exhaustion.

Long work hours.

Pressure.

Self-doubt.

The weight of responsibility.

There were days he questioned himself.

Days he wondered if all of this effort was worth it.

Days when fear of failure crept into his confidence.

On such days, I didn't motivate him.

I didn't lecture him.

I didn't give him grand speeches.

I simply reminded him of who he was.

Of what he was building.

Of the man he was becoming.

I told him,

"You don't need to be perfect.

You only need to be consistent."

And he kept going.

The third struggle came when he had to start choosing between comfort and clarity.

Some friendships had to be released.

Some habits had to be broken.

Some environments had to be left.

This was the hardest part.

Because a lot of people tolerate wrong friendships only because they fear abandonment.

They fear being alone.

They fear losing familiarity.

They fear starting over.

But the truth is simple:

If someone truly loves you —

They will never leave you because you are growing.

Friends who walk away when you rise are never friends.

They were companions of convenience.

If you tolerate nonsense in the name of loyalty,

You never grow.

And they never let you grow.

Karthik and I both realised this together:

To become a king, you must clear a lot of emotional debris.

A kingdom cannot be built on broken bricks.

Some people left his lives silently.

Some burned bridges loudly.

Some disappeared slowly.

And through every single loss,

I stood there.

Not to comfort him from pain —

But to walk him through transformation.

Because when you build a kingdom,

You don't just build walls and towers.

You break many old houses within yourself too.

And while he was building his career,

While he was losing friends,

While he was fighting his fears,

I was building my own foundation too.

We didn't compete.

We didn't rush.

We didn't cling.

We aligned.

We chose to grow in parallel —

So one day, when the world looked at us,

It wouldn't see two rebels.

It would see two individuals who built themselves so strongly that nothing superficial could shake their truth.

And somewhere deep inside, we both knew:

The day our parents come together,

It will not be because we begged.

It will be because they *saw*.

They will see the stability.

They will see maturity.

They will see the respect.

They will see the life we built —

Brick by brick.

And on that day,

Love will no longer be a question anymore.

It will be an answer.

Chapter 14

THE DIVINE ALIGNMENT

We both realised it was time at the same time.

Not because we had reached something big,

but because we were finally growing without rushing.

And with that growth came a quiet, unshakeable confidence.

The first test didn't arrive with noise.

It arrived in hesitation.

After the decision was made inside our hearts, the world didn't collapse overnight. Life moved on as usual. Our conversations were gentle. Our days continued. Our smiles stayed in place. But underneath all of it, I could feel it — we were standing at the edge of something irreversible.

One evening, Karthik grew unusually silent.

Not distant.

Not cold.

Just... quiet in a way that told me his mind was carrying weight.

When I asked gently, "What's running in your head?"

He paused for a long moment.

Then he said the words I had known would someday come:

"My parents won't take this easily."

There was no drama in his voice. Only the truth.

I didn't react. I didn't panic. I didn't argue. Healing had taught me one important thing — when a person is standing in fear, they don't need pressure. They need steadiness.

So I asked only one question.

"Do you believe in us?"

He looked at me without blinking and said,

"With everything I am."

And that was enough.

Resistance doesn't scare you when your foundation is strong.

A few days later, he told his parents.

Not with rebellion.

Not with anger.

But with respect.

He didn't say, "I will do this no matter what."

He said, "This is someone I believe in."

His mother was shocked.

Not dramatic — but visibly shaken. That silence where you can feel a storm behind the calm. Fear rushed in immediately. Not fear of me as a person — but fear of the unknown. Fear of society. Fear of judgment. Fear of losing control.

And yet, Karthik didn't sense danger.

He wasn't overconfident.

He wasn't scared either.

He was simply *certain*.

For the first time, he opened up without trembling.

She was scared. Of course, she was. Any mother would be.

But he looked at her and said softly,

"I will take care of everything.

I won't run from responsibility.

All I ask is — meet her once.

Not as my choice.

But as a person."

Then he said something that changed everything:

"I want you to meet her and *like her*. Not tolerate her."

That night when he called me, his voice was calm… but tired.

"I didn't fight," he said quietly.

"I didn't argue. I just listened. And I told them one thing — I won't force you… but I won't run from this either."

At that moment, I saw the man he was becoming.

Not aggressive.

Not submissive.

Grounded.

And for the first time in my life, I experienced something new in love:

A man didn't promise to protect me from the storm.

He chose to stand inside it with me.

Days passed.

We didn't constantly talk about the future.

Not because we were scared — but because we trusted it enough to stop clinging.

We focused on work.

On discipline.

On ourselves.

On the outside, nothing had changed yet.

On the inside, everything had.

I knew one thing with crystal clarity:

If this union was meant to break, it would have already.

The fact that it was standing quietly meant something bigger was at work.

I didn't pray for instant approval.

I didn't beg for acceptance.

I prayed only this:

"God… give him courage without hardening his heart.

Give me patience without breaking my spirit.

And if this is meant to stay… align what we cannot."

And slowly… alignment began.

Not loudly.

Not dramatically.

But in small shifts.

A question that stopped sounding angry.

A tone that softened.

A mother who listened instead of opposing.

A father who stopped refusing and started observing.

There were still walls.

But now, there were doors.

THE MYTH OF FALSE HOPE

There is something I want to say, not as advice, but as something I learned through my own life…

People talk a lot about "false hopes."
They use it so casually — almost like a warning.
But the truth is, *before even trying anything,* how can hope be false?
It's always the **effort** that matters more than the outcome.

When I look at my own journey,
if there is one thing that still fills my heart with gratitude,
it is this: **Karthik took the steps he could take.**
He showed up in the ways he knew.
He didn't run away from the process just because the result was uncertain.
And that, to me, is more beautiful than any guarantee.

We are all writing an exam called life.
We can prepare, we can show up, we can give our best…

but the results?
They are never in our hands.

So if someone asks you for something,
and your heart genuinely wants to try —
try.
Even if it doesn't work out,
you will sleep peacefully knowing you honoured your truth.

And the people who truly love you
will always understand your effort —
even if things don't go the way you hoped.

But if someone can't see your effort,
if they dismiss your time,
if they call your hope "false,"
then that person was never worth your emotional investment anyway.
It becomes a win-win either way —
you either get what you wanted
or you get the clarity you needed.

So the next time the phrase "false hope" enters your mind,
pause and ask yourself:

"Is this really false hope…
or am I just letting fear speak louder than my heart?"

Because hope is not the problem.
Fear is.
Hope moves you.
Fear freezes you.

And I learned this only after coming back to India —
that the right people don't judge your hope.
They appreciate your courage.

A few days passed by in silence

And then one day… his mother agreed to meet me Luckily.

I still remember that day vividly.

I was extremely nervous.

My hands were cold.

My heart kept racing.

I had imagined this moment so many times — but nothing prepares you for the real thing.

When I saw her, I folded my hands instinctively. My voice trembled when I spoke.

I didn't talk about caste/Religion.

I didn't talk about society.

I didn't talk about "proving myself."

I only spoke from my heart.

"Auntie," I said softly,

"I don't know what I should do for you to accept me as your daughter. But I know one thing… your son is as important to me as you are."

Her eyes widened slightly.

I continued, with my voice shaking but steady:

"I am ready to wait as long as it takes.

Just like Karthik, you are equally important to me.

I want to spend my life knowing you —

going out with you,

talking to you,

sharing my days with you,

even when he is not around."

I paused, gathered all my courage, and said:

"Even after your daughter leaves this house one day, I want to stay.

When uncle is not at home, I want you to feel you are not alone.

I don't just want to be your son's wife…

I want to be your best friend."

By then, tears were already rolling down my face.

"Please accept me.

And if you need time, let us meet again.

Please tell me what you want.

Tell me how you want me to be.

I am here."

That moment changed something.

Not entirely.

Not instantly.

But deeply.

Because she didn't see rebellion in me.

She didn't see ego.

She saw surrender with dignity.

And that is the only language a mother's heart truly understands.

When I walked out that day, I didn't know what her final answer would be.

But I knew one thing:

For the first time in my life,

I had not chased acceptance —

I had offered truth.

And Karthik?

He didn't fight for me with noise.

He fought with steadiness.

With patience.

With integrity.

And this time…

We didn't run.

What made everything even more meaningful was this —

Karthik and I came from different cultural worlds.

Different ways of celebrating.

Different food habits.

Different family rhythms.

Different emotional expressions.

Different traditions.

And yet, when we stood in front of each other, none of that felt like a barrier.

It felt like an expansion.

We didn't try to erase our differences.

We didn't try to dominate with sameness.

We chose to *understand.*

I learned his culture with curiosity, not resistance.

He learned mine with respect, not judgment.

We asked questions.

We made mistakes.

We laughed at our misunderstandings.

We corrected ourselves with softness.

There were moments where our upbringing showed up sharply.

Moments where silence felt safer than speaking.

Moments where we had to unlearn reactions that once protected us.

Moments where our families' values stood at opposite ends of the room.

But every time that happened, we didn't choose ego.

We chose *maturity.*

Maturity is not about agreeing on everything.

Maturity is about staying even when it's uncomfortable.

It is about listening when it's easier to withdraw.

It is about respecting the wound behind the reaction.

We handled every sensitive conversation slowly.

No rushed decisions.

No emotional threats.

No manipulation.

No emotional blackmail.

When fear rose, we paused.

When uncertainty appeared, we waited.

When opinions clashed, we softened.

Because both of us knew one thing with absolute clarity —

We were not fighting each other.

We were fighting *for the same future.*

There was dignity in the way we stood.

There was patience in the way we waited.

There was grace in the way we spoke.

There was faith in the way we trusted.

And slowly, everyone around us felt it.

Our families didn't see rebellion.

They saw responsibility.

They didn't see obsession.

They saw stability.

They didn't see defiance.

They saw depth.

That is the strange thing about truth —

It may be questioned at first,

But it never needs justification forever.

Over time, our relationship stopped being "a concern"

And started becoming "a conversation."

Then "an observation."

And finally, "an acceptance."

Not because we proved anyone wrong loudly —

But because we lived quietly, right.

We didn't win approval in one day.

We earned trust over time.

And when trust enters a room, fear slowly leaves.

Today, when I look back at how we handled everything —

I don't see chaos.

I see quiet strength.

I see two people who chose to grow instead of react.

I see two people who chose patience over panic.

I see two people who believed in alignment more than in force.

We didn't chase permission.

We became worthy of trust.

We didn't beg destiny.

We prepared ourselves for it.

We didn't collapse under pressure.

We stood taller inside it.

And that is why, when everything finally came together, it did not feel like a victory.

It felt like *home.*

Because what is meant for you does not arrive with fear.

It arrives with stillness.

It does not arrive with chaos.

It arrives with clarity.

It does not arrive with noise.

It arrives with quiet certainty.

And today, with the most profound humility in my heart, I can say this:

We didn't force this story.

We didn't steal it.

We didn't manipulate it.

We *grew into it.*

Through distance.

Through resistance.

Through waiting.

Through healing.

Through becoming.

And in the end…

God did it.

And this is my story.

CHAPTER 15

WHEN THE PAST RETURNED GENTLY

Whenever I look back at my journey, I feel something I never thought I would feel —

pride.

I was never a career-driven girl.

I never dreamt of climbing ladders or collecting achievements.

But life — especially my relationships — pushed me into becoming a version of myself

I didn't even know it existed.

A stronger version.

A woman with clarity.

A woman who chooses her life intentionally.

And through all the heartbreaks, goodbyes, and shifts,

one belief silently kept me going:

"There is love meant for me. Somewhere."

I didn't know who.

I didn't know when.

But I believed it.

And, just like I always say —

people from your past reappear when the timing is right,

not to restart old stories,

but to close them gracefully

or to enter your life in a different form.

That's exactly what happened when I returned to India.

THE CALL I NEVER EXPECTED

One afternoon, out of nowhere, Arjun called.

More than two years had passed since I had even seen him.

Years ago, just hearing his name would make my heart tremble —

with fear, confusion, hope, pain… everything mixed together.

But now?

Something in me was different.

Calmer.

Clearer.

More grown.

So when he said,

"Shall we meet?"

I didn't feel anxious.

I just said,

"Okay… let's meet casually."

I didn't want answers from him.

I didn't want closure.

I didn't want an apology or explanation.

I only wanted peace —

for him and for myself.

We met at a quiet café in the evening.

Warm yellow lights.

Wooden tables.

The smell of coffee and cinnamon.

People minding their own world.

When he walked in, it felt strange for exactly five seconds —

that awkwardness of two people who once knew every corner of each other's lives

But now I didn't even know whether to hug or just wave.

So we chose just to laugh and break the silence ourselves.

Once we sat down, something surprising happened —

It felt normal.

Not intense.

Not emotional.

Just… normal.

Not like how I had rehearsed it a hundred times in my mind.

I realised I had forgiven him long ago.

Not for him,

but for myself —

to free the version of me that kept carrying the weight of those memories.

I told him about Italy, about Manasa,

and eventually about Karthik —

how beautifully and naturally that bond grew.

He listened quietly.

He was happy for me.

Genuinely happy.

He told me he was dating someone, too.

Manasa had already told me,

but I let him share it in his own way.

There was no jealousy.

No comparison.

No tightness in the chest.

Just two people

who had once been everything to each other

are now sitting peacefully as friends.

I even teased him,

"Please be nice to her at least."

And we both laughed.

That laughter held closure that words could never give.

That evening, I walked out of the café with a strange lightness.

For the first time in my life,

Arjun did not belong to my "pain story."

He did not carry the weight of being my heartbreak.

He did not hold the label of "the past that broke me."

He simply returned as a person —

someone I once loved deeply,

someone who contributed to my growth,

someone who taught me important lessons,

someone who is now just a friend.

And more importantly:

Someone I wish well.

This was something I had manifested for years —

to be able to remember him

without hurting.

And it happened.

HOW KARTHIK AND ARJUN FIT INTO MY STORY

Karthik already knew Arjun — they were mutual friends long before any of this.

So nothing was awkward, nothing was hidden.

And here is what life taught me through them:

In someone's story,

Arjun may be the greatest blessing.

In someone else's story,

Karthik may be the painful memory.

We cannot tag people as "good" or "bad."

People are different versions of themselves

in different timelines

with different hearts

and different levels of awareness.

Arjun was a lesson for me —

a necessary one.

He helped me grow.

He helped me understand what I deserved.

And now, he is simply a kind friend.

Karthik, on the other hand —

It is aligned with who I am today.

More mature.

More centred.

More grounded.

We met each other at the right time

with the right intention.

One taught me what love cannot be.

One is teaching me what love should feel like.

Both stories matter.

Both shaped me.

THE MEETING I NEVER THOUGHT I'D SEE

There came a day when Karthik and Arjun met.

Nothing dramatic happened.

They were warm, respectful, and normal.

And watching them speak,

I realised something beautiful:

When trust is strong, nothing feels like a threat.

When growth is mutual, insecurity doesn't exist.

When clarity is deep, the past has no power.

Karthik and I trust each other with a level of certainty

I have never experienced this before.

When a relationship is built on that kind of clarity,

there is no space for jealousy, fear, or comparison.

Everyone has their place in my life now —

And each place feels right.

WHAT I CARRIED FORWARD

Now, when I think of Arjun,

There is no pain.

Only gratitude.

He is happy for me.

I am happy for him.

Our story found a gentle continuation —

not as lovers,

But as two people who learned,

healed,

and grew up.

Our timeline wasn't aligned for the future.

But it aligned beautifully for closure.

And that, to me,

It is one of the kindest gifts life has ever given.

CHAPTER 16

THE RISE AFTER EVERY FALL

The house was quiet, wrapped in the kind of silence that only comes when two souls are asleep under the same roof — peacefully, securely, lovingly.

And yet, I found myself awake, standing alone on the balcony of *our* home.

My home.

Our home.

The home that held both our journeys.

The home where two cultures didn't clash — they chose each other.

Where traditions didn't compete — they blended into something beautiful.

Where two families with their own histories, beliefs, fears and hopes slowly opened their hearts and said,

"Yes… let's build something good together."

That night, I stood there with the wind touching my face, the city lights stretching endlessly before me, and my entire life — every single version of myself — playing in front of my eyes.

It was past midnight.

The kind of time where thoughts become honest and hearts become loud.

I looked at the sky — the same sky that once witnessed my breakdowns, my loneliness, my begging for clarity, my confusion, my heartbreak, my fear of abandonment, my anxiety-filled nights, and those moments where I didn't recognise myself anymore.

But tonight, I stared at the same sky as a different woman altogether.

THE WOMAN WHO STOOD ON THAT BALCONY YEARS AGO

I remembered the girl I used to be — standing in a balcony somewhere else, years ago, unable to breathe, wondering why life felt so heavy, wondering why love hurt so much, wondering why nothing ever made sense.

She cried in silence.

She begged for answers.

She believed losing someone meant losing everything.

She placed people so high on a pedestal that when they wobbled,

her entire world collapsed.

That girl had dreams,

but she also had fear —

fear of being alone,

fear of not being enough,

fear of not being chosen,

fear that her worth depended on someone else's love.

And I stood there now, in the balcony of the house I share with the man I love,

realising how far I had come from her.

THE DAY TWO FAMILIES BECAME ONE

Our wedding wasn't just an event — it was a transformation.

Two cultures met, not to dominate each other, but to honour the existence of both.

There was colour everywhere — the gold of my saree, the deep maroon of his shawl, the jasmine in my hair, the sandalwood on his forehead.

The air smelled of flowers and hope.

People from two different worlds smiled at each other gently,

as if saying, *"We don't know everything about each other, but we're willing to learn."*

Karthik stood in front of me —

the man of my dreams,

my answered prayer,

the peace I had wished for every night when sleep refused to come.

Looking at him that day felt like looking directly at destiny.

The way he smiled.
The way his eyes softened when they met mine.
The way he held my hand with such certainty.
Everything in that moment said,
"You're safe. You're loved. You're chosen."
If I was ever going to marry someone,
I knew one thing with absolute clarity—
I should see *God* in that person.
Not in a religious way,
but in the purity of his character,
in the gentleness of his heart,
in the truth in his actions.
A man whose presence feels divine,
whose intentions are clean,
whose love stands tall even in storms.
I always believed that if I choose someone as my life partner,
I should be willing to fight any battle for him—
and I want him to fight with the same devotion,
the same faith,
the same unwavering strength.
Because a marriage is not just two people holding hands.
It is two souls holding destiny together.
And to hold destiny together,

you need a love that feels like prayer.

His parents accepted me wholeheartedly —

not because I was perfect,

not because I fit into every expectation,

but because they saw my sincerity,

my softness,

my willingness to grow in love.

And I promised myself that day:

"I will honour this home the way my parents honoured theirs —

with patience, dignity, effort, and warmth."

WHO STOOD WITH US

Arjun came.

Manasa came.

Friends who had seen my rise, my fall, my confusion, my healing — all of them were there.

There was no awkwardness.

No tension.

No remnants of the past.

Just peace.

Arjun congratulated me with a genuine smile —

and I realised that the universe had granted me one of my deepest wishes:

to make peace with my past completely.

Manasa stood there glowing, proud, emotional —

the friend who saw my transformation from the inside,

who knew every chapter I lived through,

who held my hand on the days I felt empty,

who reminded me of my worth when I couldn't even look at myself.

Seeing all of them together — my past, my present, my future —

made me understand one thing very clearly:

Nothing in my life was a mistake.

Nothing was wasted.

Every person, every tear, every love, every loss

was preparing me for this moment.

THE WOMAN I BECAME

As I stood in the balcony of our home,

I realised something profound:

I had risen.

Risen above heartbreak.

Above self-doubt.

Above fear.

Above my own limitations.

I didn't chase healing —

I *became* healing.

I didn't chase love —

I *became* the woman who attracts the right kind of love.

I worked on every area of my life —

my confidence,

my discipline,

my inner peace,

my emotional strength,

my stability.

And I am still growing.

Still learning.

Still evolving with humility.

Because growth is not a destination.

It's a lifestyle.

THE NIGHT I FELT IT FULLY

And that night, as I stood on the balcony,

I felt a quiet excitement inside me —

the same excitement I felt the very first time I met Karthik.

Tomorrow morning, I would wake up next to him again.

The man who walks beside me,

not ahead of me,

not behind me —

beside me.

And with that peaceful thought,

I went to bed.

For the first time in a long time,

I slept like someone whose heart had finally come home.

THE MOMENT I BECAME WHOLE

As I lay there, drifting into sleep,
a truth settled gently in my chest —
a truth I had been walking toward my whole life.

After discovering my true worth,
after learning to take people off the pedestals
I had once placed them on so blindly,
I finally understood something life-changing:

It was our love that made them special —
not the other way around.
And what is even more special…
is me.

Somewhere along this journey,
I became a vibrational match for everything I wanted.
And I realised the real power was never in beauty, approval,
or perfection.
It was always in my mind,
my courage,
and my character.

When I started vibrating at a better frequency,
people around me didn't magically transform…
but slowly, gently, steadily —

they shifted.
Life shifted.
My world shifted.

Not like a movie.
But my life *is* a movie —
one that I am directing.
A story where I write the script,
I choose the character I play,
and I promised myself
never to stop being the main character in my own life.

And then there is Karthik.

Everyone deserves a Karthik in their life —
not necessarily as a boyfriend or husband,
but as someone who holds a mirror to your worth
when you've forgotten how to see it yourself.

In my life's battles,
he stood beside me like a comrade —
quiet, steady, unwavering.
He fought his fears to stay.
He fought his patterns to grow.
He fought his hesitation to choose love.

Every day, I silently thank his mother
for raising a son with that kind of heart.
Only a queen can raise princes like that.

Together, we rose.
By being aware,
by rewiring old beliefs,
by rewriting every story that once broke me —
I rose beyond my fears.

Karthik rose beyond his fear of commitment.
I rose beyond my fear of rejection.

When he came back into my life,
I didn't run toward him out of desperation.
I simply continued paving my own path,
and life — in its quiet wisdom —
brought us back to each other
because we were finally aligned.

I rose beyond the fear of quitting
by setting small goals
and building a mind strong enough to honor them.

I rose beyond the fear of losing people
by first finding myself.

And now, standing where I stand today,
I know this with absolute clarity:

This is who I became —
a woman who rose beyond all her fears
and finally began living life fully.

So to anyone reading this,
anyone trembling on the edge of change,
anyone afraid to lose, afraid to try, afraid to love again —

Don't fear the fall.
You are not really falling.
It is the rise of the greatest beginnings —
the moment you finally understand your true power.

And I hope — with all my heart —
that you too will rise beyond all your fears
and step into the life that has been waiting for you.

ABOUT THE AUTHOR

Reshma Peela holds an MBA from the **Indian Institute of Management, Kozhikode (IIMK)** and a B.Tech in Computer Science from **GITAM University**. She currently works as a **Business Analyst**, where her interest in people, emotions, and real-world behaviour naturally aligns with her analytical work.

Alongside her professional journey, Reshma is also involved in co-building meaningful ventures such as **House of AARNI** and **LearnRIT**, where she brings together creativity, learning, and purpose. These projects reflect her belief that life becomes richer when we create things that help others grow.

Much of her inspiration comes from observing human nature — in herself and in others. Over the years, she has seen many relationships break not from lack of love, but from fear, misunderstandings, and emotional unawareness. She believes the external world is often a reflection of our inner world: our courage, our wounds, and our readiness to rise or retreat.

One unexpected meeting with her best friend transformed the way she looked at love, identity, healing, and destiny. That shift in perspective eventually became the seed for *Rise Beyond Your Fears.*

Reshma lives in Hyderabad and is currently working on multiple dreams at once — building ventures, writing, growing, and choosing to live a life grounded in love and courage.

Her hope for every reader is simple:
May you find a love that feels safe and steady.
May you meet someone who sees your worth deeply.
And may you become the version of yourself who naturally attracts that kind of love.

EPILOGUE

Rise Above Your Fears

There comes a moment in every journey when you stop asking, *"Why did this happen to me?"* and begin whispering, *"Thank you for who it made me become."*

This book was never just about the struggles, the losses, the detours, or the nights that felt too long. It was about the quiet strength that kept rising inside me — the strength that refused to give up even when everything else said I should.

Life never promised me ease.
But it promised growth, transformation, and a chance to rewrite my own story.

And I took it.
With trembling hands, stubborn hope, and a heart that still believed in love, destiny, and second chances.

If you're holding this book today, I want you to know something gently and deeply — **you are stronger than the moment you're living in.** Your fears are not the end of your story, and your pain is not the final version of you. Every setback is simply a preparation. Every ending is a quiet beginning.

I learnt that healing is not a straight path.
Some days you move forward.
Some days you stand still.
Some days you breathe through the ache.

But all of it — every step, every tear, every breakthrough — is part of becoming who you were always meant to be.

And if there is one message I want to leave you with, it is this:

You can rise.
Again and again.
Even when the world doesn't expect you to.
Even when you stop expecting it from yourself.

Because inside every fall, there is a hidden invitation — an invitation to rise higher than before.

Thank you for reading my journey.
Thank you for finding pieces of your courage in mine.

And wherever life takes you next…
may you always remember:
You are allowed to start over.
You are allowed to become new.
You are allowed to rise above your fears.

AFTERWORD

For Everyone Who Chose to Rise

If you are reading this final page,
know that this book was never meant to be just one person's story.
It is a reflection of **every heart that has broken and rebuilt**,
every soul that has loved and feared,
and every human being who has walked through darkness
only to find a new kind of light.

Most of us go through these silent battles —
the fear of losing someone,
the ache of loving deeply,
the burden of expectations,
the confusion of identity,
the longing to be understood,
and the courage it takes to keep moving forward
even when nothing makes sense.

This book was written for anyone who has ever felt that.

Not because your story looks exactly like mine,
but because your heart has felt emotions that mine has felt too:
uncertainty, hope, fear, faith, ache, and finally… awakening.

Somewhere along life, all of us learn the same truth:

Healing is not about forgetting the past —
it is about no longer living in it.

What rises from pain is not perfection,
but clarity.
Strength.
Self-respect.
And the understanding that love — real love — begins inside you.

If these pages made you pause,
or reflect,
or breathe differently,
or remember your own journey,
then this book has done what it was meant to do.

Because this story is not just mine.
It belongs to **every person who has ever tried to rise beyond fear**:
the girl who loved too much,
the boy who carried wounds quietly,
the woman who rebuilt her life,
the man who finally chose courage,
and the countless hearts that are still learning how to trust again.

As you close this book,
remember this:

You are not alone.
You are not behind.
You are not broken just because you feel deeply.
You are simply human —
and humans grow in seasons, not straight lines.

May you walk forward with courage.
May you never fear the fall.
Because every fall teaches you to rise higher.

And every rise takes you closer to the person you were always meant to become.

Your becoming has already begun.
Keep going.

ACKNOWLEDGEMENTS

This book exists because of many hearts, many conversations, and many quiet moments of support that guided me when I couldn't guide myself.

To my **family**,
Thank you for loving me in ways that gave me strength even when I didn't recognise it in myself. Your faith has always been my foundation.

To my **grandmother**,
whose presence has always felt like a blessing in my life.
You taught me how to live with grace, patience, and a full heart — lessons that shaped every chapter of who I am.

To my **best friend**,
Thank you for being the turning point I didn't know I needed.
Your presence changed the way I looked at life, love, and myself.
This book would not have been written without you being there in my life.

To the people who walked into my life at the right time —
some to stay,
some to teach,
some to remind me who I am,
and some to show me who I never want to be.
Each of you shaped a part of this story more than you'll ever realise.

To every friend who listened,
every person who trusted me with their experiences,
every conversation that made me reflect —
Thank you for helping me understand the human heart a little deeper.

To the readers who pick up this book,
Thank you for opening these pages and letting a piece of this journey sit beside yours.
If even one sentence helps you breathe differently or see yourself with more love, then this book has served its purpose.

And finally,
to the version of me who kept going —
who held on, who healed slowly, who chose courage over fear,
and who believed in love even on the days it felt impossible
—

Thank you.

Without her, none of this would exist.

Tab 28

I want to add apart where i want ti address the false hopes Which people use it a lot

Before even trying anything, there is no such thing called false hopes

Its always the efforts that matters

Even in the end when karthik and I decided to try i wouldn't have felt devastated had he tried and lost bcz the real winners are people who try when there is a chance What anyone looks at are the efforts not the result this none of us ideally decide

Let us take an example where you have decided to give an interview or an exam till the very end if you really wanna get it you will try right? Irrespective of what , if you feel like giving you never wanted it or your fears are just more than your wishes When you truly want you will try, in the end the result we all doesn't know no we all are driven by hope in life even for the smallest of the smallest things , with all the power you had you just need to try, when you use the word false hope think before it, is it because i never wanted or are my fears controlling me more than my wishes? Had karthik tried and lost i would have still been proud of him and respected him the same bcz all the effort, he would have always been a real winner